Take It to Your Seat Centers
Common Core Language 3

Common Core Language Standard CCLS	Center	Skill	Page
CCLS 3.1a	Parts of Speech	Identify, and know the function of, parts of speech in sentences	7
CCLS 3.1b	Regular and Irregular Plural Nouns	Distinguish between regular and irregular plural nouns and use irregular plural nouns in sentences	19
CCLS 3.1d	Regular and Irregular Verbs	Distinguish between regular and irregular verbs in sentences	31
CCLS 3.1e	Simple Verb Tenses	Use simple verb tenses to form complete sentences	47
CCLS 3.1f	Subject-Verb Agreement	Form sentences that have subject-verb agreement	61
CCLS 3.1f	Pronoun-Antecedent Agreement	Form sentences that have pronoun-antecedent agreement	73
CCLS 3.1h, 3.1i	Coordinating Conjunctions in Compound Sentences	Use coordinating conjunctions to complete sentences and form compound sentences	85
CCLS 3.1h, 3.1i	Subordinating Conjunctions in Complex Sentences	Use subordinating conjunctions to complete sentences and form complex sentences	97
CCLS 3.4b	Affixes	Learn common prefixes and suffixes and their meanings and identify words with the same affixes	109
CCLS 3.4c	Root Words	Match definitions to root words; identify word roots in words and use the words in context sentences	121
CCLS 3.5b	Words in Real Life	Recognize the relationship between vocabulary and real life	133
CCLS 3.5c	Shades of Meaning	Distinguish between the meanings of words used to describe thoughts and feelings	145

© Evan-Moor Corp. • EMC 2873 • Take It to Your Seat Centers—Language

Using the Centers

The 12 centers in this book provide hands-on practice to help students master standards-based language skills. It is important to teach each skill and to model the use of each center before asking students to do the tasks independently. The centers are self-contained and portable. Students can work at a desk, at a table, or on a rug, and they can use the centers as often as needed.

Why Use Centers?

- Centers are a motivating way for students to practice important skills.
- They provide for differentiated instruction.
- They support kinesthetic and visual learners.
- They can be used for teaching skills or for informal assessments.

Before Using the Centers

Here are a few things to consider:

- Will students select a center, or will you assign the centers and use them as a skill assessment tool?
- Will there be a specific block of time for centers, or will the centers be used by students throughout the day as they complete other work?
- What procedure will students use when they need help with the center tasks?
- Will students use the answer key to check their own work?

Introducing the Centers

Use the teacher instructions page and the student directions on the center's cover page to teach or review the skill. Show students the center and model how to use it as you read each step of the directions.

Recording Progress

Reproduce the Center Checklist (page 4) and use it to record the date when a student completes each center and the student's skill level.

I Can Statements

Reproduce enough *I Can* statements to give one of each to each student. Then cut apart the statements, and choose one of the options below:

Option 1: Put each statement with its corresponding center and instruct students to take one upon completion of each center.

Option 2: Distribute each statement to students after you correct and return their written practice page.

You may wish to have students display the *I Can* statements on a bulletin board, in a learning log, or in their student portfolios.

Making the Centers

Included for Each Center
- (A) Student directions/cover page
- (B) Mats and task cards
- (C) Reproducible activity
- (D) Answer key

Materials Needed
- Folders with inside pockets
- Small envelopes or self-closing plastic bags (for storing task cards)
- Pencils or marking pens (for labeling envelopes)
- Scissors
- Double-sided tape, glue stick, or stapler (for attaching the cover page to the front of the folder)
- Laminating equipment

How to Assemble and Store
1. Attach the center's cover page to the front of the folder.
2. Place reproduced activity pages in the left-hand pocket of the folder.
3. Cut apart the task cards. Then laminate the mats and task cards.
4. Cut apart the laminated task cards and put them in a labeled envelope or self-closing plastic bag. Place the mats and task cards in the right-hand pocket of the folder. If you want the centers to be self-checking, include the answer key in the folder.
5. Store prepared centers in a file box or a crate.

(D) Fold the answer key page in half, as shown. The answers for the mat activity are inside, and the answers for the reproducible activity are on the back.

Assembled Center

© Evan-Moor Corp. • EMC 2873 • Take It to Your Seat Centers—Language

Student _____ Note: Reproduce and record student progress.

Center Checklist

Center / Skill	Skill Level	Date
1. Parts of Speech Identify, and know the function of, parts of speech in sentences		
2. Regular and Irregular Plural Nouns Distinguish between regular and irregular plural nouns and use irregular plural nouns in sentences		
3. Regular and Irregular Verbs Distinguish between regular and irregular verbs in sentences		
4. Simple Verb Tenses Use simple verb tenses to form complete sentences		
5. Subject-Verb Agreement Form sentences that have subject-verb agreement		
6. Pronoun-Antecedent Agreement Form sentences that have pronoun-antecedent agreement		
7. Coordinating Conjunctions in Compound Sentences Use coordinating conjunctions to complete sentences and form compound sentences		
8. Subordinating Conjunctions in Complex Sentences Use subordinating conjunctions to complete sentences and form complex sentences		
9. Affixes Learn common prefixes and suffixes and their meanings and identify words with the same affixes		
10. Root Words Match definitions to root words; identify word roots in words and use the words in context sentences		
11. Words in Real Life Recognize the relationship between vocabulary and real life		
12. Shades of Meaning Distinguish between the meanings of words used to describe thoughts and feelings		

Note: Reproduce for each student.

I Can Statements

I can...

explain the function of parts of speech in sentences

L3.1a Parts of Speech

Conventions of Standard English | EMC 2873 © Evan-Moor Corp.

I can...

form and use regular and irregular plural nouns

L3.1b Regular and Irregular Plural Nouns

Conventions of Standard English | EMC 2873 © Evan-Moor Corp.

I can...

form and use regular and irregular verbs

L3.1d Regular and Irregular Verbs

Conventions of Standard English | EMC 2873 © Evan-Moor Corp.

I can...

form and use the simple verb tenses

L3.1e Simple Verb Tenses

Conventions of Standard English | EMC 2873 © Evan-Moor Corp.

I can...

form sentences that have subject-verb agreement

L3.1f Subject-Verb Agreement

Conventions of Standard English | EMC 2873 © Evan-Moor Corp.

I can...

form sentences that have pronoun-antecedent agreement

L3.1f Pronoun-Antecedent Agreement

Conventions of Standard English | EMC 2873 © Evan-Moor Corp.

© Evan-Moor Corp. • EMC 2873 • *Take It to Your Seat Centers—Language*

Note: Reproduce for each student.

I Can Statements

I can...
use coordinating conjunctions and form compound sentences

L3.1h, L3.1i   Coordinating Conjunctions
Conventions of Standard English | EMC 2873 © Evan-Moor Corp.

I can...
use subordinating conjunctions and form complex sentences

L3.1h, L3.1i   Subordinating Conjunctions
Conventions of Standard English | EMC 2873 © Evan-Moor Corp.

I can...
know the meaning of the new word formed when a known affix is added to a known word

L3.4b   Affixes
Vocabulary Acquisition and Use | EMC 2873 © Evan-Moor Corp.

I can...
use a known root word as a clue to the meaning of an unknown word with the same root

L3.4c   Root Words
Vocabulary Acquisition and Use | EMC 2873 © Evan-Moor Corp.

I can...
identify real-life connections between words and their use

L3.5b   Words in Real Life
Vocabulary Acquisition and Use | EMC 2873 © Evan-Moor Corp.

I can...
distinguish shades of meaning among related words used to describe thoughts and feelings

L3.5c   Shades of Meaning
Vocabulary Acquisition and Use | EMC 2873 © Evan-Moor Corp.

Take It to Your Seat Centers

Parts of Speech

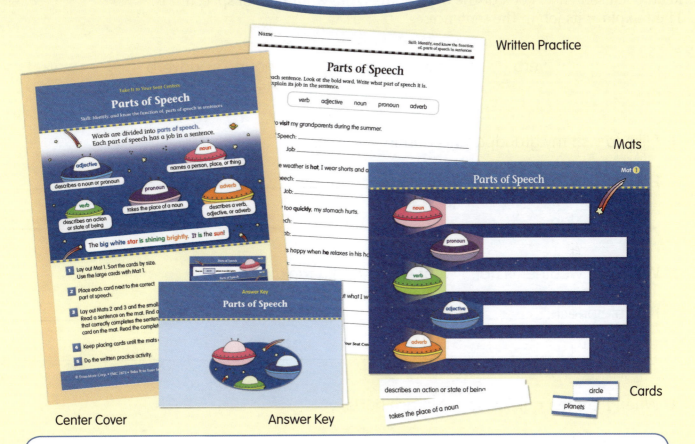

Written Practice

Mats

Cards

Center Cover

Answer Key

CCLS 3.1a Explain the function of nouns, pronouns, verbs, adjectives, and adverbs in general and their functions in particular sentences

Skill: Identify, and know the function of, parts of speech in sentences

Steps to Follow

1. **Prepare the center.** (See page 3.)
2. **Introduce the center.** State the goal. Say: *You will use different parts of speech to complete sentences. Then you will explain the function of the different parts of speech.*
3. **Teach the skill.** Demonstrate how to use the center.
4. **Practice the skill.** Have students complete the center tasks independently or with a partner.

Contents

Written Practice..... 8

Center Cover.......... 9

Answer Key............ 11

Center Mats 13

Cards 17

Name _____

Skill: Identify, and know the function of, parts of speech in sentences

Parts of Speech

Read each sentence. Look at the bold word. Write what part of speech it is. Then explain its job in the sentence.

> verb   adjective   noun   pronoun   adverb

1. I like to **visit** my grandparents during the summer.

    Part of Speech: _____

    Job: _____

2. When the weather is **hot**, I wear shorts and a tank top.

    Part of Speech: _____

    Job: _____

3. When I eat too **quickly**, my stomach hurts.

    Part of Speech: _____

    Job: _____

4. My grandpa is happy when **he** relaxes in his hammock.

    Part of Speech: _____

    Job: _____

5. I like to lie in the **grass** and think about what I will do when I grow up.

    Part of Speech: _____

    Job: _____

Take It to Your Seat Centers

Parts of Speech

Skill: Identify, and know the function of, parts of speech in sentences

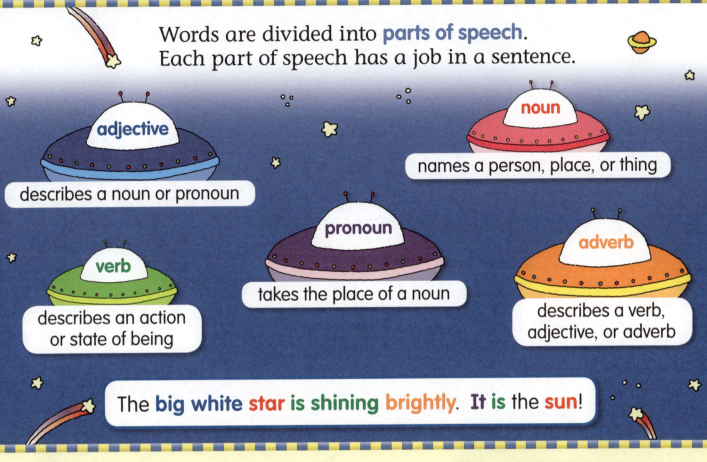

1. Lay out Mat 1. Sort the cards by size. Use the large cards with Mat 1.

2. Place each card next to the correct part of speech.

3. Lay out Mats 2 and 3 and the small cards. Read a sentence on the mat. Find a word card that correctly completes the sentence. Place the card on the mat. Read the completed sentence.

4. Keep placing cards until the mats are complete.

5. Do the written practice activity.

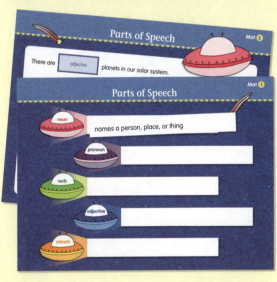

Parts of Speech

Answer Key

Written Practice

Name _____

Skill: Identify and know the function of parts of speech in sentences

Parts of Speech

Read each sentence. Look at the bold word. Write what part of speech it is. Then explain its job in the sentence.

verb   adjective   noun   pronoun   adverb

1. I like to **visit** my grandparents during the summer.
   Part of speech: **verb**
   Job: **describes an action or state of being**

2. When the weather is **hot**, I wear shorts and a tank top.
   Part of speech: **adjective**
   Job: **describes a noun or pronoun**

3. When I eat too **quickly**, my stomach hurts.
   Part of speech: **adverb**
   Job: **describes a verb, an adjective, or an adverb**

4. My grandpa is happy when **he** relaxes in his hammock.
   Part of speech: **pronoun**
   Job: **takes the place of a noun**

5. I like to lie in the **grass** and think about what I will do when I grow up.
   Part of speech: **noun**
   Job: **names a person, place, or thing**

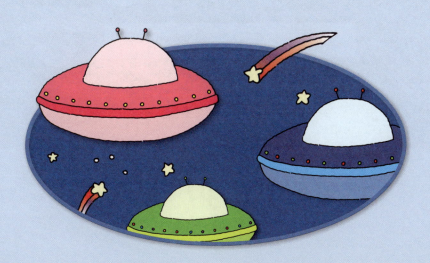

Answer Key

Parts of Speech

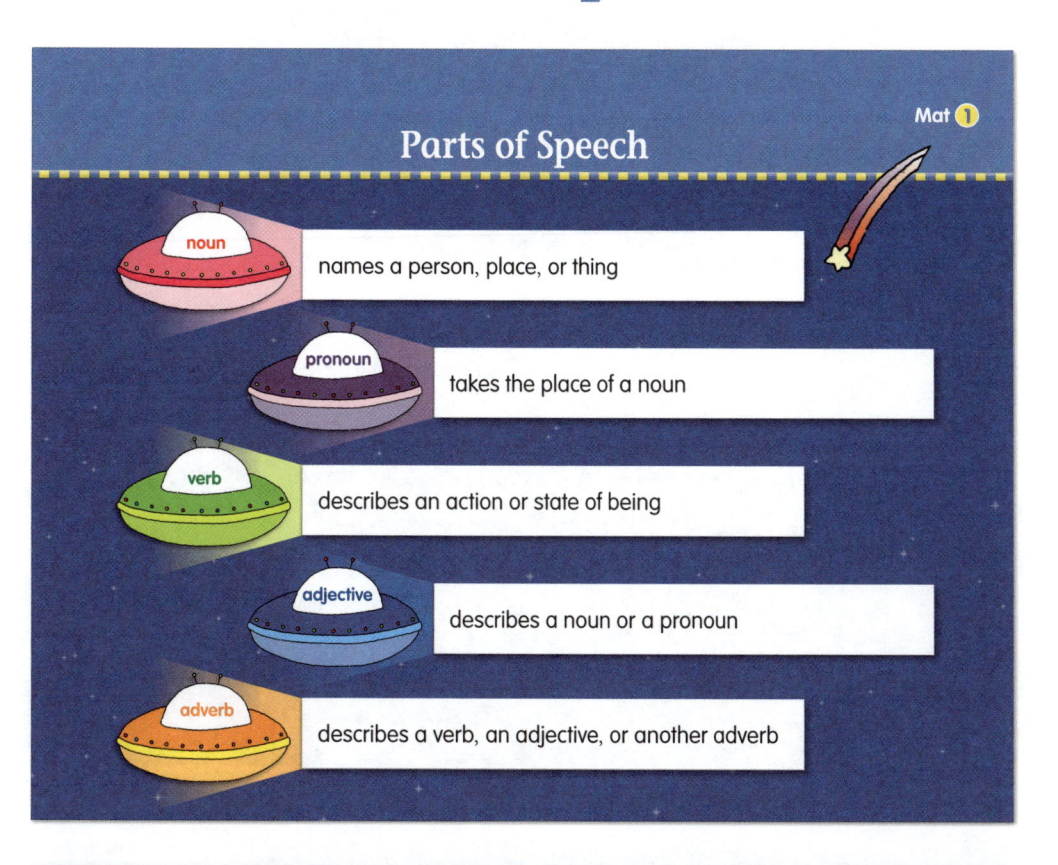

Parts of Speech — Mat 1

noun — names a person, place, or thing

pronoun — takes the place of a noun

verb — describes an action or state of being

adjective — describes a noun or a pronoun

adverb — describes a verb, an adjective, or another adverb

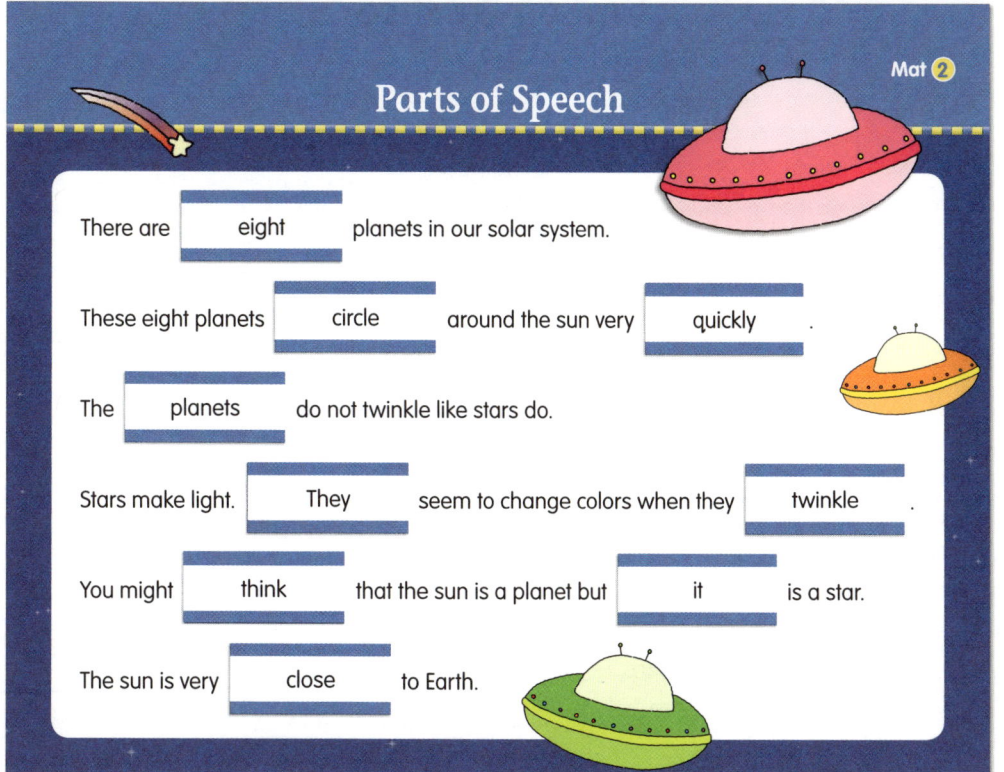

Parts of Speech — Mat 2

There are **eight** planets in our solar system.

These eight planets **circle** around the sun very **quickly**.

The **planets** do not twinkle like stars do.

Stars make light. **They** seem to change colors when they **twinkle**.

You might **think** that the sun is a planet but **it** is a star.

The sun is very **close** to Earth.

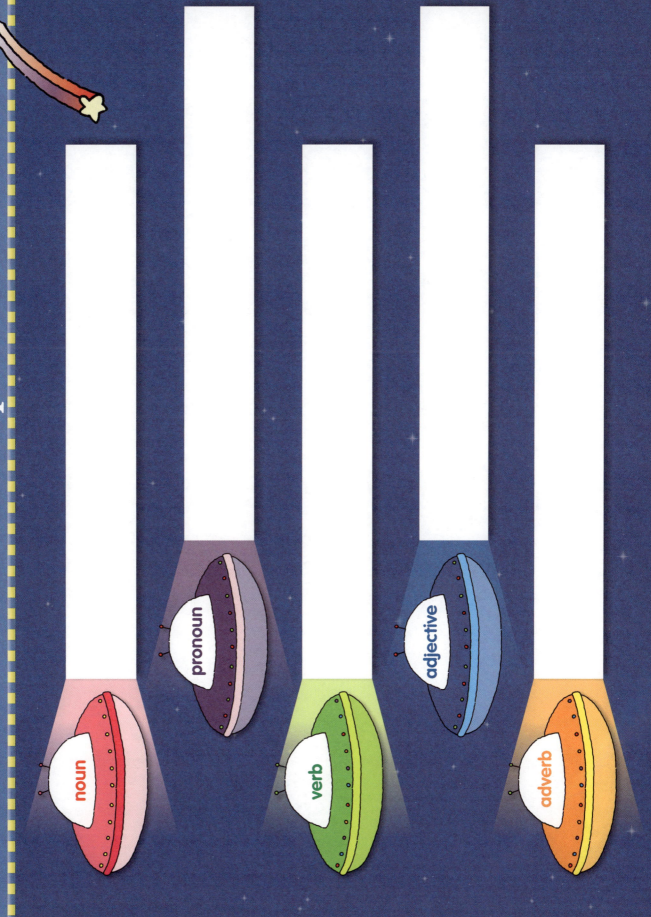

Parts of Speech

There are [adjective] planets in our solar system.

These eight planets [verb] around the sun very [adverb].

The [noun] do not twinkle like stars do.

Stars make light. [pronoun] seem to change colors when they [verb].

You might [verb] that the sun is a planet but [pronoun] is a star.

The sun is very [adjective] to Earth.

Mat 2

Cards for Mat 1

names a person, place, or thing

takes the place of a noun

describes an action or state of being

describes a noun or a pronoun

describes a verb, an adjective, or another adverb

Cards for Mat 2

eight	circle	quickly
planets	They	twinkle
think	it	close

Parts of Speech
EMC 2873
© Evan-Moor Corp.

Parts of Speech
EMC 2873
© Evan-Moor Corp.

Parts of Speech
EMC 2873
© Evan-Moor Corp.

Parts of Speech
EMC 2873
© Evan-Moor Corp.

Parts of Speech
EMC 2873
© Evan-Moor Corp.

Parts of Speech **EMC 2873** © Evan-Moor Corp.	Parts of Speech **EMC 2873** © Evan-Moor Corp.	Parts of Speech **EMC 2873** © Evan-Moor Corp.
Parts of Speech **EMC 2873** © Evan-Moor Corp.	Parts of Speech **EMC 2873** © Evan-Moor Corp.	Parts of Speech **EMC 2873** © Evan-Moor Corp.
Parts of Speech **EMC 2873** © Evan-Moor Corp.	Parts of Speech **EMC 2873** © Evan-Moor Corp.	Parts of Speech **EMC 2873** © Evan-Moor Corp.

Take It to Your Seat Centers
Regular and Irregular Plural Nouns

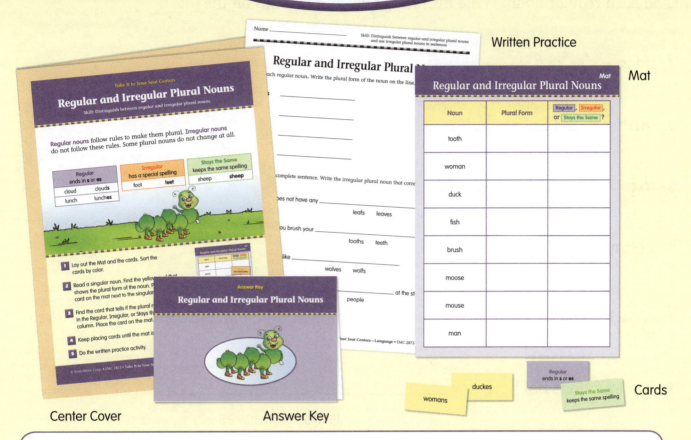

CCLS 3.1b Form and use regular and irregular plural nouns

Skill: Distinguish between regular and irregular plural nouns and use irregular plural nouns in sentences

Steps to Follow

1. **Prepare the center.** (See page 3.)

2. **Introduce the center.** State the goal. Say: *You will read each noun, find a card that shows the plural form, and then decide if the plural form of the noun is regular, irregular, or the same.*

3. **Teach the skill.** Demonstrate how to use the center.

4. **Practice the skill.** Have students complete the center tasks independently or with a partner.

Contents

Written Practice..... 20

Center Cover.......... 21

Answer Key............ 23

Center Mat............. 25

Cards 27

Name _____

Skill: Distinguish between regular and irregular plural nouns and use irregular plural nouns in sentences

Regular and Irregular Plural Nouns

Read each regular noun. Write the plural form of the noun on the line.

1. **boss** _____

2. **bush** _____

3. **fox** _____

4. **penny** _____

Read each incomplete sentence. Write the irregular plural noun that correctly completes the sentence.

5. The tree does not have any _____.
                               leafs   leaves

6. Make sure you brush your _____ after you eat.
                               tooths   teeth

7. My dogs look like _____.
                           wolves   wolfs

8. There are lots of _____ at the store.
                           persons   people

Take It to Your Seat Centers

Regular and Irregular Plural Nouns

Skill: Distinguish between regular and irregular plural nouns

Regular nouns follow rules to make them plural. **Irregular nouns** do not follow these rules. Some plural nouns do not change at all.

Regular ends in **s** or **es**	
cloud	cloud**s**
lunch	lunch**es**

Irregular has a special spelling	
foot	**feet**

Stays the Same keeps the same spelling	
sheep	**sheep**

1. Lay out the Mat and the cards. Sort the cards by color.

2. Read a singular noun. Find the yellow card that shows the plural form of the noun. Place the card on the mat next to the singular noun.

3. Find the card that tells if the plural noun goes in the Regular, Irregular, or Stays the Same column. Place the card on the mat.

4. Keep placing cards until the mat is complete.

5. Do the written practice activity.

Written Practice

Regular and Irregular Plural Nouns

Read each regular noun. Write the plural form of the noun on the line.

1. boss — **bosses**
2. bush — **bushes**
3. fox — **foxes**
4. penny — **pennies**

Read each incomplete sentence. Write the irregular plural noun that correctly completes the sentence.

5. The tree does not have any **leaves**. — leafs / leaves
6. Make sure you brush your **teeth** after you eat. — tooths / teeth
7. My dogs look like **wolves**. — wolfs / wolves
8. There are lots of **people** at the store. — persons / people

---

Answer Key
Regular and Irregular Plural Nouns

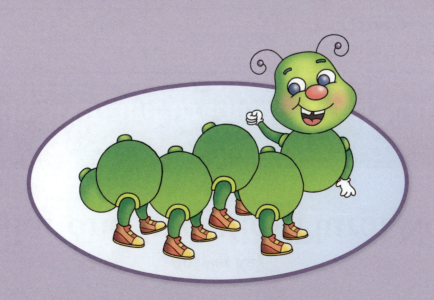

Answer Key

Regular and Irregular Plural Nouns

Regular and Irregular Plural Nouns

Mat

Noun	Plural Form	Regular, Irregular, or Stays the Same?
tooth	teeth	**Irregular** has a special spelling
woman	women	**Irregular** has a special spelling
duck	ducks	**Regular** ends in **s** or **es**
fish	fish	**Stays the Same** keeps the same spelling
brush	brushes	**Regular** ends in **s** or **es**
moose	moose	**Stays the Same** keeps the same spelling
mouse	mice	**Irregular** has a special spelling
man	men	**Irregular** has a special spelling

Regular and Irregular Plural Nouns

Mat

Noun	Plural Form	Regular, Irregular, or Stays the Same?
tooth		
woman		
duck		
fish		
brush		
moose		
mouse		
man		

Cards

tooths	teeth	womans
women	duckes	ducks
fishes	fish	brushes
brushs	mooses	moose
mouses	mice	mans
men		

Regular and Irregular Plural Nouns

EMC 2873

© Evan-Moor Corp.

Regular and Irregular Plural Nouns

EMC 2873

© Evan-Moor Corp.

Regular and Irregular Plural Nouns

EMC 2873

© Evan-Moor Corp.

Regular and Irregular Plural Nouns

EMC 2873

© Evan-Moor Corp.

Regular and Irregular Plural Nouns

EMC 2873

© Evan-Moor Corp.

Regular and Irregular Plural Nouns

EMC 2873

© Evan-Moor Corp.

Regular and Irregular Plural Nouns

EMC 2873

© Evan-Moor Corp.

Regular and Irregular Plural Nouns

EMC 2873

© Evan-Moor Corp.

Regular and Irregular Plural Nouns

EMC 2873

© Evan-Moor Corp.

Regular and Irregular Plural Nouns

EMC 2873

© Evan-Moor Corp.

Regular and Irregular Plural Nouns

EMC 2873

© Evan-Moor Corp.

Regular and Irregular Plural Nouns

EMC 2873

© Evan-Moor Corp.

Regular and Irregular Plural Nouns

EMC 2873

© Evan-Moor Corp.

Regular and Irregular Plural Nouns

EMC 2873

© Evan-Moor Corp.

Regular and Irregular Plural Nouns

EMC 2873

© Evan-Moor Corp.

Regular and Irregular Plural Nouns

EMC 2873

© Evan-Moor Corp.

Cards

Regular ends in **s** or **es**	Irregular has a special spelling	Stays the Same keeps the same spelling
Regular ends in **s** or **es**	Irregular has a special spelling	Stays the Same keeps the same spelling
Regular ends in **s** or **es**	Irregular has a special spelling	Stays the Same keeps the same spelling
Regular ends in **s** or **es**	Irregular has a special spelling	Stays the Same keeps the same spelling

Regular and Irregular Plural Nouns	Regular and Irregular Plural Nouns	Regular and Irregular Plural Nouns
EMC 2873 © Evan-Moor Corp.	EMC 2873 © Evan-Moor Corp.	EMC 2873 © Evan-Moor Corp.
Regular and Irregular Plural Nouns	Regular and Irregular Plural Nouns	Regular and Irregular Plural Nouns
EMC 2873 © Evan-Moor Corp.	EMC 2873 © Evan-Moor Corp.	EMC 2873 © Evan-Moor Corp.
Regular and Irregular Plural Nouns	Regular and Irregular Plural Nouns	Regular and Irregular Plural Nouns
EMC 2873 © Evan-Moor Corp.	EMC 2873 © Evan-Moor Corp.	EMC 2873 © Evan-Moor Corp.
Regular and Irregular Plural Nouns	Regular and Irregular Plural Nouns	Regular and Irregular Plural Nouns
EMC 2873 © Evan-Moor Corp.	EMC 2873 © Evan-Moor Corp.	EMC 2873 © Evan-Moor Corp.

Take It to Your Seat Centers

Regular and Irregular Verbs

Written Practice

Mats

Center Cover

Answer Key

Cards

CCLS 3.1d Form and use regular and irregular verbs

Skill: Distinguish between regular and irregular verbs and use regular and irregular verbs in sentences

Steps to Follow

1. **Prepare the center.** (See page 3.)

2. **Introduce the center.** State the goal. Say: *You will match present tense and past tense verbs and label them as regular or irregular.*

3. **Teach the skill.** Demonstrate how to use the center.

4. **Practice the skill.** Have students complete the center tasks independently or with a partner.

Contents

Written Practice..... 32

Center Cover.......... 33

Answer Key............ 35

Center Mats........... 37

Cards..................... 41

© Evan-Moor Corp. • EMC 2873 • Take It to Your Seat Centers—Language   **Teacher Instructions** 31

Name _____

Skill: Write sentences using regular and irregular verbs

Regular and Irregular Verbs

Read each **regular verb**. Write a sentence using the **past tense** form of the verb.

1. play _____

2. help _____

3. talk _____

Read each **irregular verb**. Write a sentence using the **past tense** form of the verb.

4. buy _____

5. break _____

6. swim _____

Take It to Your Seat Centers

Regular and Irregular Verbs

Skill: Distinguish between regular and irregular verbs

Most verbs are **regular** verbs. You follow a rule to make past tense verbs. Some verbs do not follow these rules. They are called **irregular verbs**.

Regular Verbs		Irregular Verbs	
present	past	present	irregular past
walk	walked	drink	drank
grab	grabbed	fight	fought
cry	cried	win	won

1. Lay out Mats 1 and 2. Sort the cards by color.

2. Use the green cards and the orange cards to match present tense verbs with past tense verbs.

3. Then place a blue card to show if the verb is regular or irregular.

4. Keep placing the cards until the mats are complete.

5. Do the written practice activity.

© Evan-Moor Corp. • EMC 2873 • Take It to Your Seat Centers—Language   Center Cover 33

Written Practice

Name _____

Skill: Write sentences using regular and irregular verbs

Regular and Irregular Verbs

Answers will vary—Examples:

Read each regular verb. Write a sentence using the past tense form of the verb.

1. **play** — We played catch at the park.

2. **help** — My dad helped me with my homework.

3. **talk** — I talked to my aunt Sara yesterday.

Read each irregular verb. Write a sentence using the past tense form of the verb.

4. **buy** — Mike bought new boots so that he could ride a horse.

5. **break** — Jason broke his arm when he fell off his bike.

6. **swim** — Lucy swam quickly across the pool.

(fold)

Answer Key

Regular and Irregular Verbs

Answer Key

Regular and Irregular Verbs

Regular and Irregular Verbs — Mat ❶

Present Tense Verb	Past Tense Verb	Regular or Irregular Verb?
play	played	Regular Verb
catch	caught	Irregular Verb
come	came	Irregular Verb
hike	hiked	Regular Verb
fly	flew	Irregular Verb
dance	danced	Regular Verb
bake	baked	Regular Verb

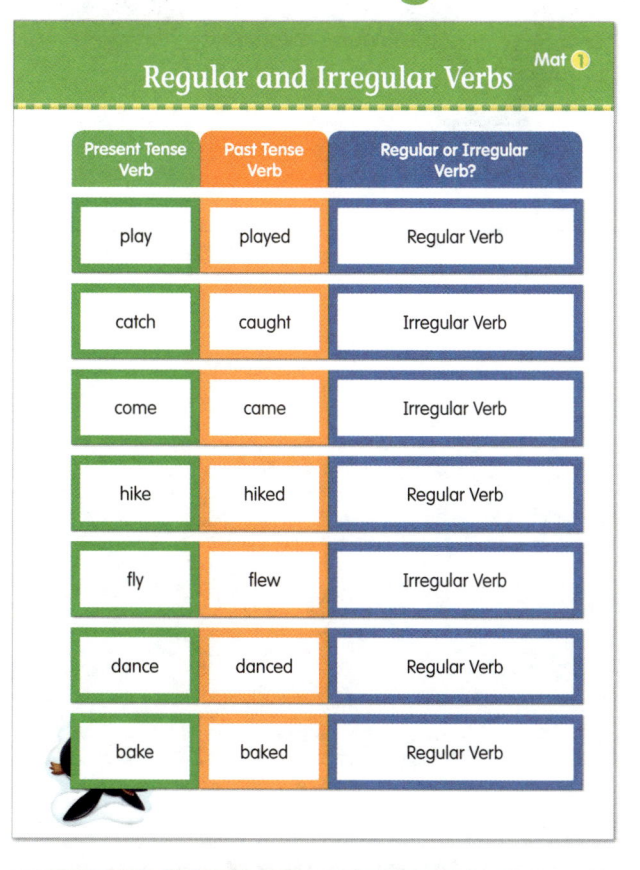

Regular and Irregular Verbs — Mat ❷

Present Tense Verb	Past Tense Verb	Regular or Irregular Verb?
speak	spoke	Irregular Verb
take	took	Irregular Verb
buy	bought	Irregular Verb
talk	talked	Regular Verb
jump	jumped	Regular Verb
give	gave	Irregular Verb
blow	blew	Irregular Verb

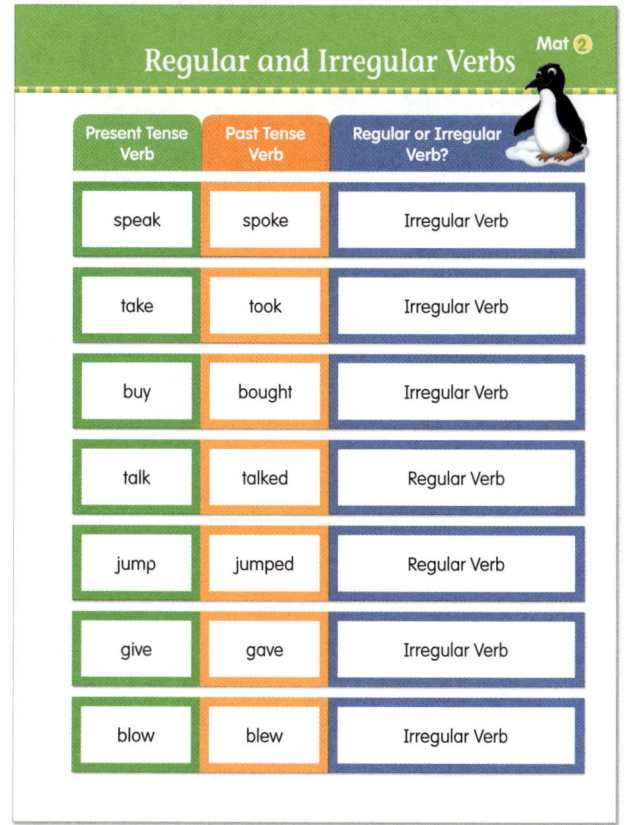

Regular and Irregular Verbs

Mat 1

Present Tense Verb	Past Tense Verb	Regular or Irregular Verb?

Regular and Irregular Verbs

Mat 2

Present Tense Verb	Past Tense Verb	Regular or Irregular Verb?

Cards for Mats 1 and 2

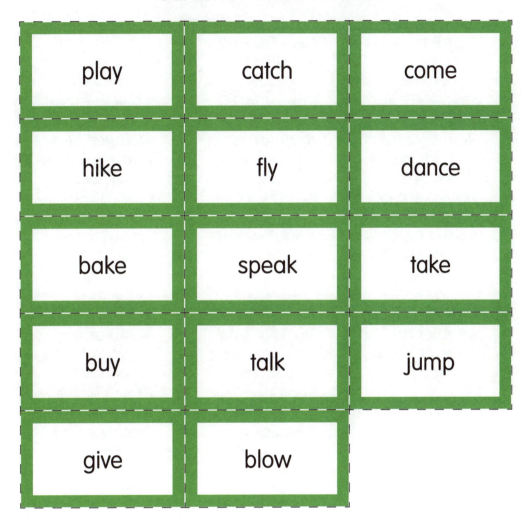

Regular and Irregular Verbs	Regular and Irregular Verbs	Regular and Irregular Verbs
EMC 2873 © Evan-Moor Corp.	EMC 2873 © Evan-Moor Corp.	EMC 2873 © Evan-Moor Corp.
Regular and Irregular Verbs EMC 2873 © Evan-Moor Corp.	**Regular and Irregular Verbs** EMC 2873 © Evan-Moor Corp.	**Regular and Irregular Verbs** EMC 2873 © Evan-Moor Corp.
Regular and Irregular Verbs EMC 2873 © Evan-Moor Corp.	**Regular and Irregular Verbs** EMC 2873 © Evan-Moor Corp.	**Regular and Irregular Verbs** EMC 2873 © Evan-Moor Corp.
Regular and Irregular Verbs EMC 2873 © Evan-Moor Corp.	**Regular and Irregular Verbs** EMC 2873 © Evan-Moor Corp.	**Regular and Irregular Verbs** EMC 2873 © Evan-Moor Corp.
	Regular and Irregular Verbs EMC 2873 © Evan-Moor Corp.	**Regular and Irregular Verbs** EMC 2873 © Evan-Moor Corp.

Cards for Mats 1 and 2

played	caught	came
hiked	flew	danced
baked	spoke	took
bought	talked	jumped
gave	blew	

Regular and Irregular Verbs	Regular and Irregular Verbs	Regular and Irregular Verbs
EMC 2873 © Evan-Moor Corp.	EMC 2873 © Evan-Moor Corp.	EMC 2873 © Evan-Moor Corp.
Regular and Irregular Verbs EMC 2873 © Evan-Moor Corp.	Regular and Irregular Verbs EMC 2873 © Evan-Moor Corp.	Regular and Irregular Verbs EMC 2873 © Evan-Moor Corp.
Regular and Irregular Verbs EMC 2873 © Evan-Moor Corp.	Regular and Irregular Verbs EMC 2873 © Evan-Moor Corp.	Regular and Irregular Verbs EMC 2873 © Evan-Moor Corp.
Regular and Irregular Verbs EMC 2873 © Evan-Moor Corp.	Regular and Irregular Verbs EMC 2873 © Evan-Moor Corp.	Regular and Irregular Verbs EMC 2873 © Evan-Moor Corp.
	Regular and Irregular Verbs EMC 2873 © Evan-Moor Corp.	Regular and Irregular Verbs EMC 2873 © Evan-Moor Corp.

Cards for Mats 1 and 2

Regular Verb	Irregular Verb
Regular Verb	Irregular Verb
Regular Verb	Irregular Verb
Regular Verb	Irregular Verb
Regular Verb	Irregular Verb
Regular Verb	Irregular Verb
Regular Verb	Irregular Verb
Regular Verb	Irregular Verb

Regular and Irregular Verbs
EMC 2873
© Evan-Moor Corp.

Regular and Irregular Verbs
EMC 2873
© Evan-Moor Corp.

Regular and Irregular Verbs
EMC 2873
© Evan-Moor Corp.

Regular and Irregular Verbs
EMC 2873
© Evan-Moor Corp.

Regular and Irregular Verbs
EMC 2873
© Evan-Moor Corp.

Regular and Irregular Verbs
EMC 2873
© Evan-Moor Corp.

Regular and Irregular Verbs
EMC 2873
© Evan-Moor Corp.

Regular and Irregular Verbs
EMC 2873
© Evan-Moor Corp.

Regular and Irregular Verbs
EMC 2873
© Evan-Moor Corp.

Regular and Irregular Verbs
EMC 2873
© Evan-Moor Corp.

Regular and Irregular Verbs
EMC 2873
© Evan-Moor Corp.

Regular and Irregular Verbs
EMC 2873
© Evan-Moor Corp.

Regular and Irregular Verbs
EMC 2873
© Evan-Moor Corp.

Regular and Irregular Verbs
EMC 2873
© Evan-Moor Corp.

Regular and Irregular Verbs
EMC 2873
© Evan-Moor Corp.

Regular and Irregular Verbs
EMC 2873
© Evan-Moor Corp.

Take It to Your Seat Centers

Simple Verb Tenses

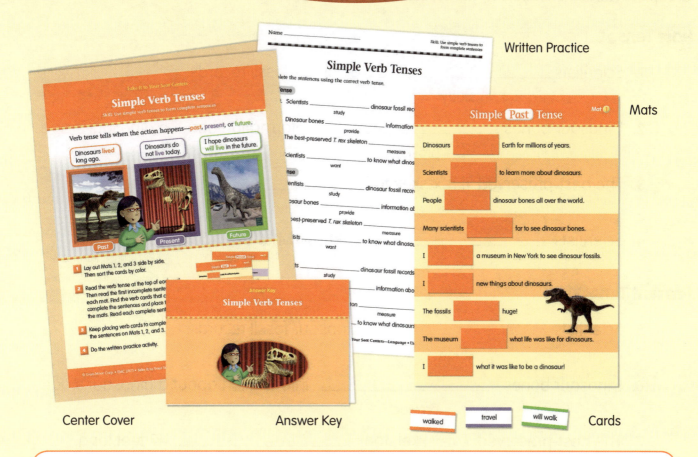

CCLS 3.1e Form and use the simple verb tenses

Skill: Use simple verb tenses to form complete sentences

Steps to Follow

1. **Prepare the center.** (See page 3.)

2. **Introduce the center.** State the goal. Say: *You will form sentences using simple verb tenses.*

3. **Teach the skill.** Demonstrate how to use the center.

4. **Practice the skill.** Have students complete the center tasks independently or with a partner.

Contents

Written Practice..... 48

Center Cover.......... 49

Answer Key............ 51

Center Mats........... 53

Cards 59

Name _____

Skill: Use simple verb tenses to form complete sentences

Simple Verb Tenses

Complete the sentences using the correct verb tense.

Past Tense

1. Scientists _____ dinosaur fossil records.
   study

2. Dinosaur bones _____ information about a dinosaur's age.
   provide

3. The best-preserved *T. rex* skeleton _____ 42 feet long.
   measure

4. Scientists _____ to know what dinosaurs looked like.
   want

Present Tense

5. Scientists _____ dinosaur fossil records.
   study

6. Dinosaur bones _____ information about a dinosaur's age.
   provide

7. The best-preserved *T. rex* skeleton _____ 42 feet long.
   measure

8. Scientists _____ to know what dinosaurs looked like.
   want

Future Tense

9. Scientists _____ dinosaur fossil records.
   study

10. Dinosaur bones _____ information about a dinosaur's age.
    provide

11. The best-preserved *T. rex* skeleton _____ 42 feet long.
    measure

12. Scientists _____ to know what dinosaurs looked like.
    want

Take It to Your Seat Centers

Simple Verb Tenses

Skill: Use simple verb tenses to form complete sentences

Verb tense tells when the action happens—**past**, **present**, or **future**.

| Dinosaurs **lived** long ago. | Dinosaurs do not **live** today. | I hope dinosaurs **will live** in the future. |

Past — Present — Future

1. Lay out Mats 1, 2, and 3 side by side. Then sort the cards by color.

2. Read the verb tense at the top of each mat. Then read the first incomplete sentence on each mat. Find the verb cards that correctly complete the sentences and place them on the mats. Read each complete sentence.

3. Keep placing verb cards to complete the sentences on Mats 1, 2, and 3.

4. Do the written practice activity.

Center Cover

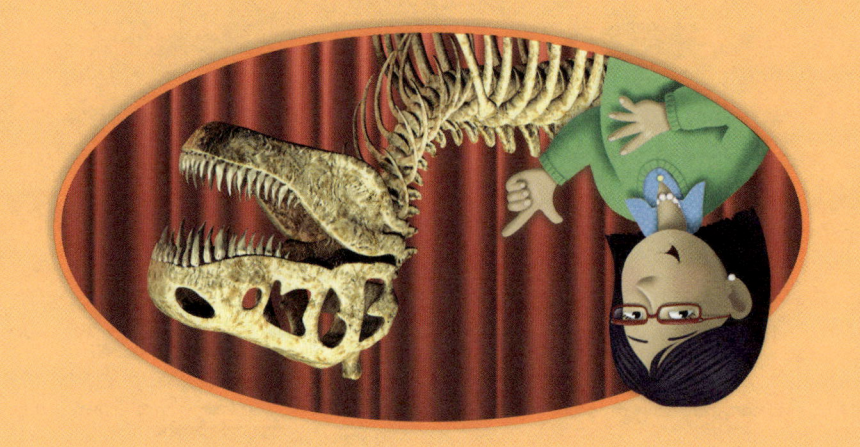

Simple Verb Tenses

Answer Key

(fold)

Written Practice

Name _____

Skill: Use simple verb tenses to form complete sentences

Simple Verb Tenses

Complete the sentences using the correct verb tense.

Past Tense

1. Scientists ___studied___ dinosaur fossil records.
study
2. Dinosaur bones ___provided___ information about a dinosaur's age.
provide
3. The best-preserved *T. rex* skeleton ___measured___ 42 feet long.
measure
4. Scientists ___wanted___ to know what dinosaurs looked like.
want

Present Tense

5. Scientists ___study___ dinosaur fossil records.
study
6. Dinosaur bones ___provide___ information about a dinosaur's age.
provide
7. The best-preserved *T. rex* skeleton ___measures___ 42 feet long.
measure
8. Scientists ___want___ to know what dinosaurs looked like.
want

Future Tense

9. Scientists ___will study___ dinosaur fossil records.
study
10. Dinosaur bones ___will provide___ information about a dinosaur's age.
provide
11. The best-preserved *T. rex* skeleton ___will measure___ 42 feet long.
measure
12. Scientists ___will want___ to know what dinosaurs looked like.
want

48 Written Practice   Take It to Your Seat Centers—Language • EMC 2873 • © Evan-Moor Corp.

Take It to Your Seat Centers—Language • EMC 2873 • © Evan-Moor Corp.

Answer Key

Simple Verb Tenses

Mat 1 — Simple Past Tense

- Dinosaurs **walked** Earth for millions of years.
- Scientists **worked** to learn more about dinosaurs.
- People **discovered** dinosaur bones all over the world.
- Many scientists **traveled** far to see dinosaur bones.
- I **visited** a museum in New York to see dinosaur fossils.
- I **learned** new things about dinosaurs.
- The fossils **looked** huge!
- The museum **showed** what life was like for dinosaurs.
- I **imagined** what it was like to be a dinosaur!

Mat 2 — Simple Present Tense

- Dinosaurs do not **walk** Earth today.
- Scientists **work** to learn more about dinosaurs.
- People **discover** dinosaur bones all over the world.
- Many scientists **travel** far to see dinosaur bones.
- I **visit** a museum in New York to see dinosaur fossils.
- I **learn** new things about dinosaurs.
- The fossils **look** huge!
- The museum **shows** what life was like for dinosaurs.
- I **imagine** what it was like to be a dinosaur!

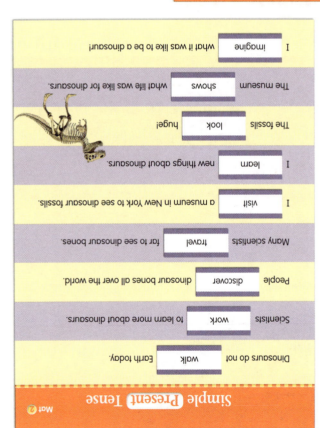

Mat 3 — Simple Future Tense

- Maybe dinosaurs **will walk** Earth millions of years from now.
- Scientists **will work** to learn more about dinosaurs.
- People **will discover** dinosaur bones all over the world.
- Many scientists **will travel** far to see dinosaur bones.
- I **will visit** a museum in New York to see dinosaur fossils.
- I **will learn** new things about dinosaurs.
- The fossils **will look** huge!
- The museum **will show** what life was like for dinosaurs.
- I **will imagine** what it was like to be a dinosaur!

Simple Past Tense

Mat 1

Dinosaurs _____ Earth for millions of years.

Scientists _____ to learn more about dinosaurs.

People _____ dinosaur bones all over the world.

Many scientists _____ far to see dinosaur bones.

I _____ a museum in New York to see dinosaur fossils.

I _____ new things about dinosaurs.

The fossils _____ huge!

The museum _____ what life was like for dinosaurs.

I _____ what it was like to be a dinosaur!

Simple Present Tense

Mat 2

Dinosaurs do not _____ Earth today.

Scientists _____ to learn more about dinosaurs.

People _____ dinosaur bones all over the world.

Many scientists _____ far to see dinosaur bones.

I _____ a museum in New York to see dinosaur fossils.

I _____ new things about dinosaurs.

The fossils _____ huge!

The museum _____ what life was like for dinosaurs.

I _____ what it was like to be a dinosaur!

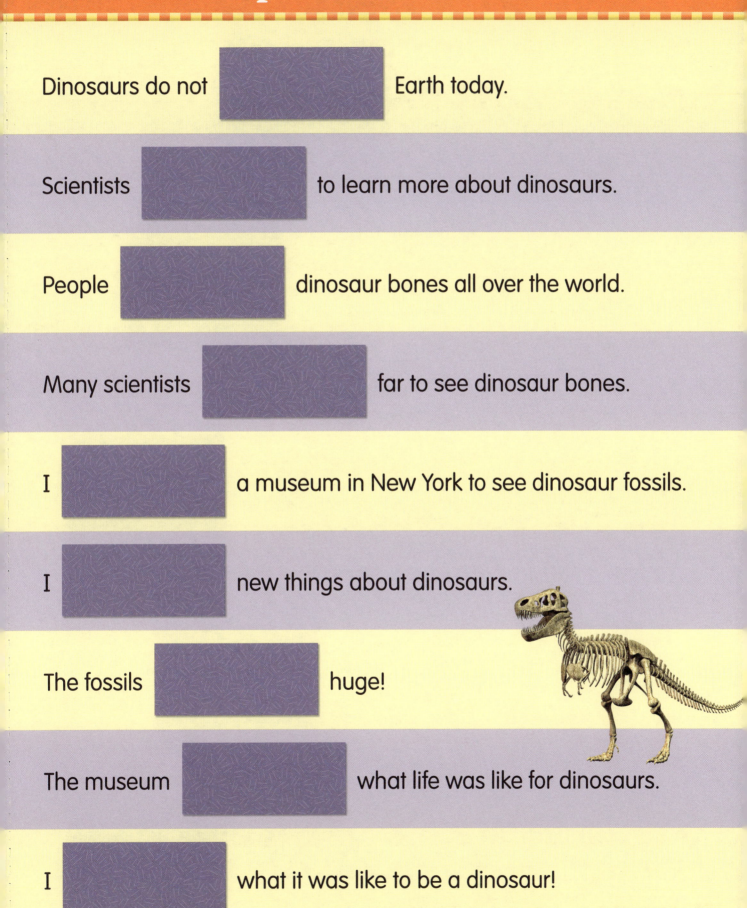

Simple Future Tense

Mat 3

Maybe dinosaurs _____ Earth millions of years from now.

Scientists _____ to learn more about dinosaurs.

People _____ dinosaur bones all over the world.

Many scientists _____ far to see dinosaur bones.

I _____ a museum in New York to see dinosaur fossils.

I _____ new things about dinosaurs.

The fossils _____ huge!

The museum _____ what life was like for dinosaurs.

I _____ what it was like to be a dinosaur!

Cards for Mat 1

walked	worked	discovered
traveled	visited	learned
looked	showed	imagined

Cards for Mat 2

walk	work	discover
travel	visit	learn
look	show	imagine

Cards for Mat 3

will walk	will work	will discover
will travel	will visit	will learn
will look	will show	will imagine

Simple Verb Tenses EMC 2873 © Evan-Moor Corp.	**Simple Verb Tenses** EMC 2873 © Evan-Moor Corp.	**Simple Verb Tenses** EMC 2873 © Evan-Moor Corp.
Simple Verb Tenses EMC 2873 © Evan-Moor Corp.	**Simple Verb Tenses** EMC 2873 © Evan-Moor Corp.	**Simple Verb Tenses** EMC 2873 © Evan-Moor Corp.
Simple Verb Tenses EMC 2873 © Evan-Moor Corp.	**Simple Verb Tenses** EMC 2873 © Evan-Moor Corp.	**Simple Verb Tenses** EMC 2873 © Evan-Moor Corp.
Simple Verb Tenses EMC 2873 © Evan-Moor Corp.	**Simple Verb Tenses** EMC 2873 © Evan-Moor Corp.	**Simple Verb Tenses** EMC 2873 © Evan-Moor Corp.
Simple Verb Tenses EMC 2873 © Evan-Moor Corp.	**Simple Verb Tenses** EMC 2873 © Evan-Moor Corp.	**Simple Verb Tenses** EMC 2873 © Evan-Moor Corp.
Simple Verb Tenses EMC 2873 © Evan-Moor Corp.	**Simple Verb Tenses** EMC 2873 © Evan-Moor Corp.	**Simple Verb Tenses** EMC 2873 © Evan-Moor Corp.
Simple Verb Tenses EMC 2873 © Evan-Moor Corp.	**Simple Verb Tenses** EMC 2873 © Evan-Moor Corp.	**Simple Verb Tenses** EMC 2873 © Evan-Moor Corp.
Simple Verb Tenses EMC 2873 © Evan-Moor Corp.	**Simple Verb Tenses** EMC 2873 © Evan-Moor Corp.	**Simple Verb Tenses** EMC 2873 © Evan-Moor Corp.
Simple Verb Tenses EMC 2873 © Evan-Moor Corp.	**Simple Verb Tenses** EMC 2873 © Evan-Moor Corp.	**Simple Verb Tenses** EMC 2873 © Evan-Moor Corp.

Take It to Your Seat Centers
Subject-Verb Agreement

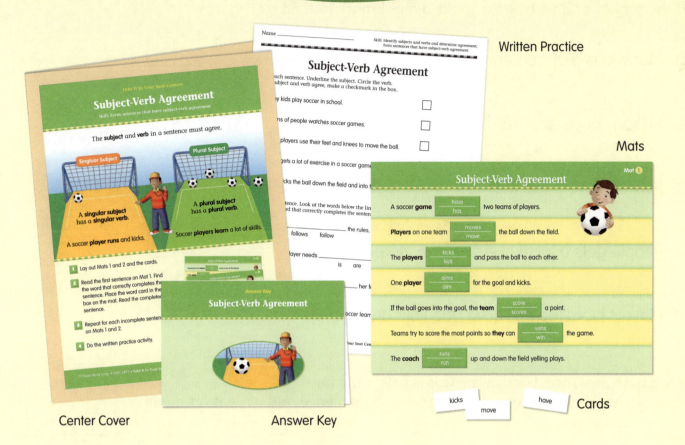

CCLS 3.1f Ensure subject-verb agreement

Skill: Form sentences that have subject-verb agreement; identify subjects and verbs and determine agreement

Steps to Follow

1. **Prepare the center.** (See page 3.)
2. **Introduce the center.** State the goal. Say: *You will place cards on mats to form sentences that have correct subject and verb agreement.*
3. **Teach the skill.** Demonstrate how to use the center.
4. **Practice the skill.** Have students complete the center tasks independently or with a partner.

Contents

Written Practice..... 62

Center Cover.......... 63

Answer Key............ 65

Center Mats........... 67

Cards..................... 71

Subject-Verb Agreement

Read each sentence. Underline the subject. Circle the verb.
If the subject and verb agree, make a checkmark in the box.

1. Many kids play soccer in school. ☐

2. Millions of people watches soccer games. ☐

3. Soccer players use their feet and knees to move the ball. ☐

4. People gets a lot of exercise in a soccer game. ☐

5. Players kicks the ball down the field and into the net. ☐

Read each sentence. Look at the words below the line.
Choose the word that correctly completes the sentence and write it on the line.

6. If players _____ the rules, soccer is an easy game to play.
   follows   follow

7. All a soccer player needs _____ a ball, a field, and two goals.
   is   are

8. A soccer player _____ her feet to move the ball.
   uses   using

9. Kids who _____ soccer learn many important skills.
   plays   play

Take It to Your Seat Centers

Subject-Verb Agreement

Skill: Form sentences that have subject-verb agreement

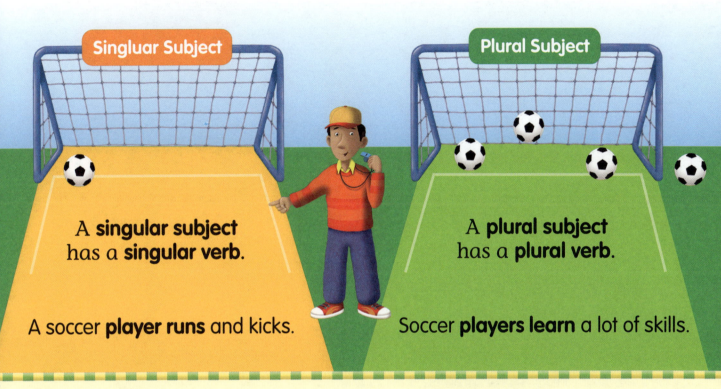

The **subject** and **verb** in a sentence must agree.

Singluar Subject

A **singular subject** has a **singular verb**.

A soccer **player runs** and kicks.

Plural Subject

A **plural subject** has a **plural verb**.

Soccer **players learn** a lot of skills.

1. Lay out Mats 1 and 2 and the cards.
2. Read the first sentence on Mat 1. Find the word that correctly completes the sentence. Place the word card in the box on the mat. Read the completed sentence.
3. Repeat for each incomplete sentence on Mats 1 and 2.
4. Do the written practice activity.

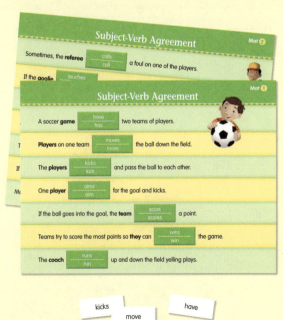

Subject-Verb Agreement

Answer Key

Written Practice

Subject-Verb Agreement

Read each sentence. Underline the subject. Circle the verb. If the subject and verb agree, make a checkmark in the box.

1. Many <u>kids</u> (play) soccer in school. ✓
2. <u>Millions of people</u> (watches) soccer games. ☐
3. <u>Soccer players</u> (use) their feet and knees to move the ball. ✓
4. <u>People</u> (gets) a lot of exercise in a soccer game. ☐
5. <u>Players</u> (kicks) the ball down the field and into the net. ☐

Read each sentence. Look at the words below the line. Choose the word that correctly completes the sentence and write it on the line.

6. If players **Follow** the rules, soccer is an easy game to play.
   follows   follow

7. All a soccer player needs **is** a ball, a field, and two goals.
   is   are

8. A soccer player **uses** her feet to move the ball.
   uses   using

9. Kids who **play** soccer learn many important skills.
   plays   play

Answer Key

Subject-Verb Agreement

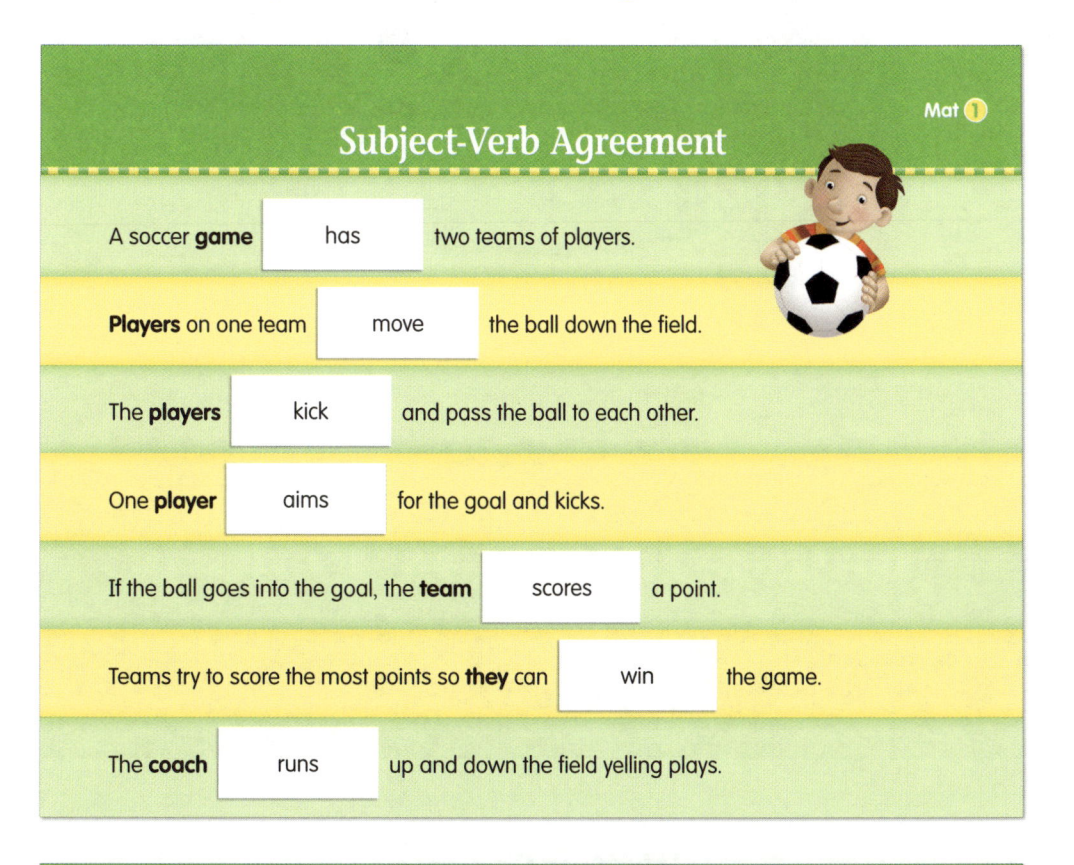

Subject-Verb Agreement
Mat ❶

A soccer **game** has two teams of players.

Players on one team move the ball down the field.

The **players** kick and pass the ball to each other.

One **player** aims for the goal and kicks.

If the ball goes into the goal, the **team** scores a point.

Teams try to score the most points so **they** can win the game.

The **coach** runs up and down the field yelling plays.

Subject-Verb Agreement
Mat ❷

Sometimes, the **referee** calls a foul on one of the players.

If the **goalie** touches the ball with his or her hands, there is no penalty.

If other players touch the ball with their hands, **they** get a penalty.

Most of the players follow the rules and enjoy playing the game.

The **fans** cheer for their favorite players.

If you've never been to a soccer game, **you** might not know how much fun they are.

Most **cities** have soccer teams for kids from age four to age eighteen.

Subject-Verb Agreement

A soccer **game** ___(have/has)___ two teams of players.

Players on one team ___(moves/move)___ the ball down the field.

The **players** ___(kicks/kick)___ and pass the ball to each other.

One **player** ___(aims/aim)___ for the goal and kicks.

If the ball goes into the goal, the **team** ___(score/scores)___ a point.

Teams try to score the most points so **they** can ___(wins/win)___ the game.

The **coach** ___(runs/run)___ up and down the field yelling plays.

Subject-Verb Agreement

Sometimes, the **referee** _calls / call_ a foul on one of the players.

If the **goalie** _touches / touch_ the ball with his or her hands, there is no penalty.

If other players touch the ball with their hands, **they** _gets / get_ a penalty.

Most of the players follow the rules and _enjoys / enjoy_ playing the game.

The **fans** _cheers / cheer_ for their favorite players.

If you've never been to a soccer game, **you** might not _knows / know_ how much fun they are.

Most **cities** _have / has_ soccer teams for kids from age four to age eighteen.

Cards for Mats 1 and 2

has	have	move	moves
kick	kicks	aims	aim
scores	score	win	wins
run	runs	call	calls
touches	touch	get	gets
enjoy	enjoys	cheer	cheers
know	knows	has	have

Subject-Verb Agreement	Subject-Verb Agreement	Subject-Verb Agreement	Subject-Verb Agreement
EMC 2873 © Evan-Moor Corp.	EMC 2873 © Evan-Moor Corp.	EMC 2873 © Evan-Moor Corp.	EMC 2873 © Evan-Moor Corp.
Subject-Verb Agreement	Subject-Verb Agreement	Subject-Verb Agreement	Subject-Verb Agreement
EMC 2873 © Evan-Moor Corp.	EMC 2873 © Evan-Moor Corp.	EMC 2873 © Evan-Moor Corp.	EMC 2873 © Evan-Moor Corp.
Subject-Verb Agreement	Subject-Verb Agreement	Subject-Verb Agreement	Subject-Verb Agreement
EMC 2873 © Evan-Moor Corp.	EMC 2873 © Evan-Moor Corp.	EMC 2873 © Evan-Moor Corp.	EMC 2873 © Evan-Moor Corp.
Subject-Verb Agreement	Subject-Verb Agreement	Subject-Verb Agreement	Subject-Verb Agreement
EMC 2873 © Evan-Moor Corp.	EMC 2873 © Evan-Moor Corp.	EMC 2873 © Evan-Moor Corp.	EMC 2873 © Evan-Moor Corp.
Subject-Verb Agreement	Subject-Verb Agreement	Subject-Verb Agreement	Subject-Verb Agreement
EMC 2873 © Evan-Moor Corp.	EMC 2873 © Evan-Moor Corp.	EMC 2873 © Evan-Moor Corp.	EMC 2873 © Evan-Moor Corp.
Subject-Verb Agreement	Subject-Verb Agreement	Subject-Verb Agreement	Subject-Verb Agreement
EMC 2873 © Evan-Moor Corp.	EMC 2873 © Evan-Moor Corp.	EMC 2873 © Evan-Moor Corp.	EMC 2873 © Evan-Moor Corp.
Subject-Verb Agreement	Subject-Verb Agreement	Subject-Verb Agreement	Subject-Verb Agreement
EMC 2873 © Evan-Moor Corp.	EMC 2873 © Evan-Moor Corp.	EMC 2873 © Evan-Moor Corp.	EMC 2873 © Evan-Moor Corp.

Take It to Your Seat Centers
Pronoun-Antecedent Agreement

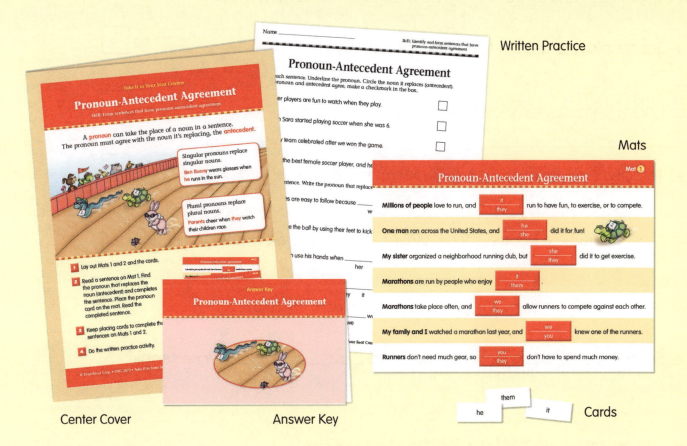

CCLS 3.1f Ensure pronoun-antecedent agreement

Skill: Identify and form sentences that have pronoun-antecedent agreement

Steps to Follow

1. **Prepare the center.** (See page 3.)

2. **Introduce the center.** State the goal. Say: *You will place cards on mats to form sentences that have correct pronoun and antecedent agreement.*

3. **Teach the skill.** Demonstrate how to use the center.

4. **Practice the skill.** Have students complete the center tasks independently or with a partner.

Contents

Written Practice..... 74

Center Cover.......... 75

Answer Key............ 77

Center Mats 79

Cards 83

Name _____

Skill: Identify and form sentences that have pronoun-antecedent agreement

Pronoun-Antecedent Agreement

Read each sentence. Underline the pronoun. Circle the noun it replaces (antecedent). If the pronoun and antecedent agree, make a checkmark in the box.

1. Soccer players are fun to watch when they play. ☐

2. Coach Sara started playing soccer when she was 6. ☐

3. The city team celebrated after we won the game. ☐

4. Mary is the best female soccer player, and he scored many goals. ☐

Read each sentence. Write the pronoun that replaces the noun.

5. Soccer rules are easy to follow because _____ are simple.
   we   they

6. Players move the ball by using their feet to kick _____.
   it   them

7. The goalie can use his hands when _____ guards the goal.
   her   he

8. Kids who love soccer can play _____ all year long.
   they   it

9. My friends and I cheer as _____ watch our team play.
   you   we

74 Written Practice   Take It to Your Seat Centers—Language • EMC 2873 • © Evan-Moor Corp.

Take It to Your Seat Centers

Pronoun-Antecedent Agreement

Skill: Form sentences that have pronoun-antecedent agreement

A **pronoun** can take the place of a noun in a sentence.
The pronoun must agree with the noun it's replacing, the **antecedent**.

Singular pronouns replace singular nouns.

Ben Bunny wears glasses when **he** runs in the sun.

Plural pronouns replace plural nouns.

Parents cheer when **they** watch their children race.

1 Lay out Mats 1 and 2 and the cards.

2 Read a sentence on Mat 1. Find the pronoun that replaces the noun (antecedent) and completes the sentence. Place the pronoun card on the mat. Read the completed sentence.

3 Keep placing cards to complete the sentences on Mats 1 and 2.

4 Do the written practice activity.

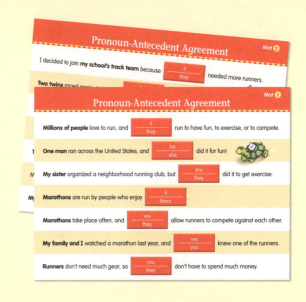

© Evan-Moor Corp. • EMC 2873 • Take It to Your Seat Centers—Language

Center Cover 75

Pronoun-Antecedent Agreement

Answer Key

(fold)

Written Practice

Name _____   Skill: Identify and form sentences that have
                                                   pronoun-antecedent agreement

Pronoun-Antecedent Agreement

Read each sentence. Underline the pronoun. Circle the noun it replaces (antecedent).
If the pronoun and antecedent agree, make a checkmark in the box.

1. Soccer (players) are fun to watch when <u>they</u> play. ☑

2. (Coach Sara) started playing soccer when <u>she</u> was 6. ☑

3. The city (team) celebrated after <u>we</u> won the game. ☐

4. (Mary) is the best female soccer player, and <u>he</u> scored many goals. ☐

Read each sentence. Write the pronoun that replaces the noun.

5. Soccer rules are easy to follow because ____**they**____ are simple.

     we   they

6. Players move the ball by using their feet to kick ____**it**____.

     it   them

7. The goalie can use his hands when ____**he**____ guards the goal.

     her   he

8. Kids who love soccer can play ____**it**____ all year long.

     they   it

9. My friends and I cheer as ____**we**____ watch our team play.

     you   we

74 Written Practice   Take It to Your Seat Centers—Language • EMC 2873 • © Evan-Moor Corp.

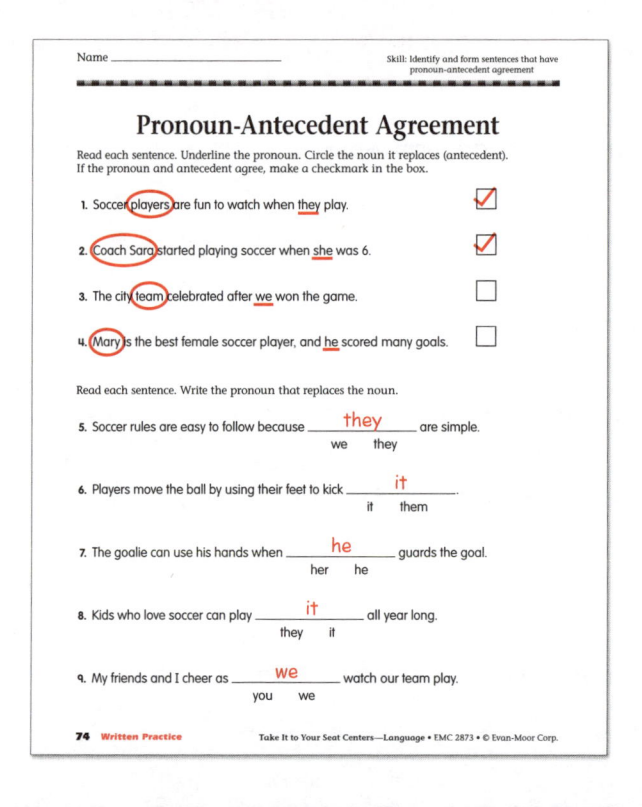

Take It to Your Seat Centers—Language • EMC 2873 • © Evan-Moor Corp.

Answer Key

Pronoun-Antecedent Agreement

Pronoun-Antecedent Agreement

Mat ❶

Millions of people love to run, and [they] run to have fun, to exercise, or to compete.

One man ran across the United States, and [he] did it for fun!

My sister organized a neighborhood running club, but [she] did it to get exercise.

Marathons are run by people who enjoy [them].

Marathons take place often, and [they] allow runners to compete against each other.

My family and I watched a marathon last year, and [we] knew one of the runners.

Runners don't need much gear, so [they] don't have to spend much money.

Pronoun-Antecedent Agreement

Mat ❷

I decided to join **my school's track team** because [it] needed more runners.

Two twins raced against me, and [they] were hard to beat.

When **Coach Reyez** said I had the best time, [he] sounded surprised!

Every day, **my teammates and I** went to track practice, where [we] worked hard.

The girls promised to do the best [they] could at every race.

My dad records **my races** and watches [them] with me when I get home.

My brother agreed to join the track team next year after [he] stops playing soccer.

Mat 1

Pronoun-Antecedent Agreement

Millions of people love to run, and ___(it/they)___ run to have fun, to exercise, or to compete.

One man ran across the United States, and ___(he/she)___ did it for fun!

My sister organized a neighborhood running club, but ___(she/they)___ did it to get exercise.

Marathons are run by people who enjoy ___(it/them)___.

Marathons take place often, and ___(we/they)___ allow runners to compete against each other.

My family and I watched a marathon last year, and ___(we/you)___ knew one of the runners.

Runners don't need much gear, so ___(you/they)___ don't have to spend much money.

Mat 2

Pronoun-Antecedent Agreement

I decided to join **my school's track team** because [it / they] needed more runners.

Two twins raced against me, and [they / you] were hard to beat.

When **Coach Reyez** said I had the best time, [he / they] sounded surprised!

Every day, **my teammates and I** went to track practice, where [we / you] worked hard.

The girls promised to do the best [they / I] could at every race.

My dad records **my races** and watches [them / him] with me when I get home.

My brother agreed to join the track team next year after [they / he] stops playing soccer.

Cards for Mats 1 and 2

it	they	he	she
she	they	it	them
we	they	we	you
you	they	it	they
they	you	he	they
we	you	they	I
them	him	they	he

Pronoun-Antecedent Agreement	Pronoun-Antecedent Agreement	Pronoun-Antecedent Agreement	Pronoun-Antecedent Agreement
EMC 2873 © Evan-Moor Corp.	EMC 2873 © Evan-Moor Corp.	EMC 2873 © Evan-Moor Corp.	EMC 2873 © Evan-Moor Corp.
Pronoun-Antecedent Agreement	Pronoun-Antecedent Agreement	Pronoun-Antecedent Agreement	Pronoun-Antecedent Agreement
EMC 2873 © Evan-Moor Corp.	EMC 2873 © Evan-Moor Corp.	EMC 2873 © Evan-Moor Corp.	EMC 2873 © Evan-Moor Corp.
Pronoun-Antecedent Agreement	Pronoun-Antecedent Agreement	Pronoun-Antecedent Agreement	Pronoun-Antecedent Agreement
EMC 2873 © Evan-Moor Corp.	EMC 2873 © Evan-Moor Corp.	EMC 2873 © Evan-Moor Corp.	EMC 2873 © Evan-Moor Corp.
Pronoun-Antecedent Agreement	Pronoun-Antecedent Agreement	Pronoun-Antecedent Agreement	Pronoun-Antecedent Agreement
EMC 2873 © Evan-Moor Corp.	EMC 2873 © Evan-Moor Corp.	EMC 2873 © Evan-Moor Corp.	EMC 2873 © Evan-Moor Corp.
Pronoun-Antecedent Agreement	Pronoun-Antecedent Agreement	Pronoun-Antecedent Agreement	Pronoun-Antecedent Agreement
EMC 2873 © Evan-Moor Corp.	EMC 2873 © Evan-Moor Corp.	EMC 2873 © Evan-Moor Corp.	EMC 2873 © Evan-Moor Corp.
Pronoun-Antecedent Agreement	Pronoun-Antecedent Agreement	Pronoun-Antecedent Agreement	Pronoun-Antecedent Agreement
EMC 2873 © Evan-Moor Corp.	EMC 2873 © Evan-Moor Corp.	EMC 2873 © Evan-Moor Corp.	EMC 2873 © Evan-Moor Corp.
Pronoun-Antecedent Agreement	Pronoun-Antecedent Agreement	Pronoun-Antecedent Agreement	Pronoun-Antecedent Agreement
EMC 2873 © Evan-Moor Corp.	EMC 2873 © Evan-Moor Corp.	EMC 2873 © Evan-Moor Corp.	EMC 2873 © Evan-Moor Corp.

Take It to Your Seat Centers

Coordinating Conjunctions in Compound Sentences

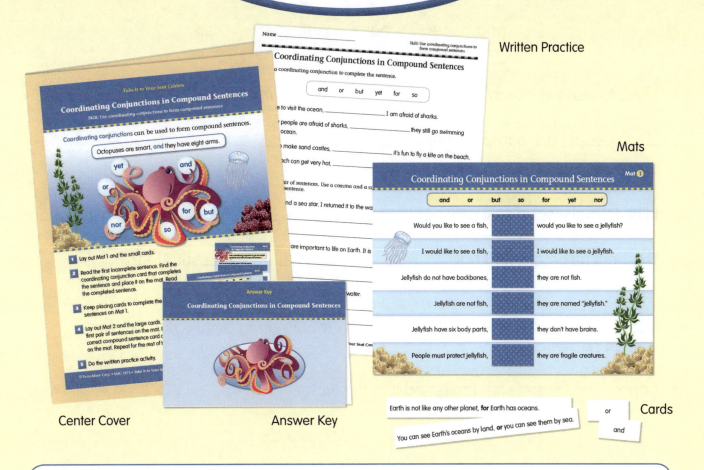

Center Cover

Answer Key

Written Practice

Mats

Cards

CCLS 3.1h, 3.1i Use coordinating conjunctions; produce compound sentences

Skill: Use coordinating conjunctions to form compound sentences

Steps to Follow

1. **Prepare the center.** (See page 3.)

2. **Introduce the center.** State the goal. Say: *You will use coordinating conjunctions to join sentences.*

3. **Teach the skill.** Demonstrate how to use the center.

4. **Practice the skill.** Have students complete the center tasks independently or with a partner.

Contents

Written Practice..... 86

Center Cover.......... 87

Answer Key............ 89

Center Mats 91

Cards 95

Name _____

Skill: Use coordinating conjunctions to form compound sentences

Coordinating Conjunctions in Compound Sentences

Write a coordinating conjunction to complete the sentence.

> and   or   but   yet   for   so

1. I love to visit the ocean, _____ I am afraid of sharks.

2. Many people are afraid of sharks, _____ they still go swimming in the ocean.

3. I like to make sand castles, _____ it's fun to fly a kite on the beach.

4. The beach can get very hot, _____ I make sure I take water.

Read each pair of sentences. Use a comma and a coordinating conjunction to write a compound sentence.

5. I once found a sea star. I returned it to the water.

   _____

   _____

6. Sea animals are important to life on Earth. It is important to protect them.

   _____

   _____

7. Sea animals are colorful. They live in water.

   _____

   _____

Take It to Your Seat Centers

Coordinating Conjunctions in Compound Sentences

Skill: Use coordinating conjunctions to form compound sentences

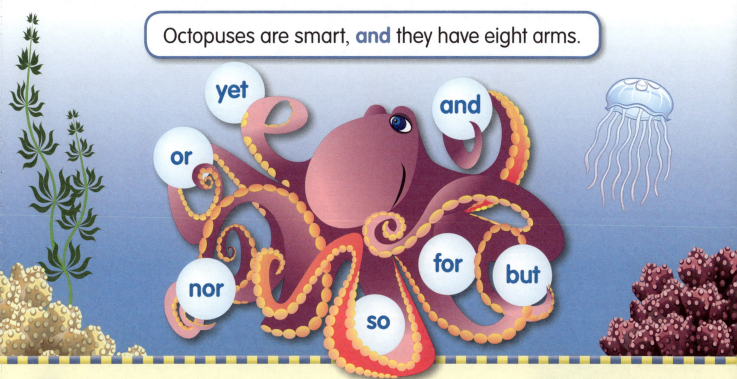

Coordinating conjunctions can be used to form compound sentences.

Octopuses are smart, **and** they have eight arms.

yet • and • or • nor • so • for • but

1 Lay out Mat 1 and the small cards.

2 Read the first incomplete sentence. Find the coordinating conjunction card that completes the sentence and place it on the mat. Read the completed sentence.

3 Keep placing cards to complete the sentences on Mat 1.

4 Lay out Mat 2 and the large cards. Read the first pair of sentences on the mat. Find the correct compound sentence card and place it on the mat. Repeat for the rest of the sentences.

5 Do the written practice activity.

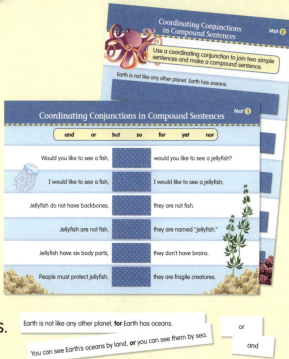

© Evan-Moor Corp. • EMC 2873 • Take It to Your Seat Centers—Language — Center Cover 87

Coordinating Conjunctions in Compound Sentences

Written Practice

Name _____

Skill: Use coordinating conjunctions to form compound sentences

Coordinating Conjunctions in Compound Sentences

Write a coordinating conjunction to complete the sentence.

| and | or | but | yet | for | so |

1. I love to visit the ocean. **but** I am afraid of sharks.
2. Many people are afraid of sharks, **yet** they still go swimming in the ocean.
3. I like to fly a kite on the beach, **and** it's fun to make sand castles.
4. The beach can get very hot, **so** I make sure I take water.

Read each pair of sentences. Use a comma and a coordinating conjunction to write a compound sentence.

5. I once found a sea star. I returned it to the water.
   I once found a sea star, but I returned it to the water.

6. Sea animals are important to life on Earth. It is important to protect them.
   Sea animals are important to life on Earth, so it is important to protect them.

7. Sea animals are colorful. They live in water.
   Sea animals are colorful, and they live in water.

Answer Key

Coordinating Conjunctions in Compound Sentences

Answer Key

Coordinating Conjunctions in Compound Sentences

Mat 1 — Coordinating Conjunctions in Compound Sentences

| and | or | but | so | for | yet | nor |

- Would you like to see a fish. / or / would you like to see a jellyfish?
- I would like to see a fish. / and / I would like to see a jellyfish.
- Jellyfish do not have backbones, / so / they are not fish.
- Jellyfish are not fish, / yet / they are named "jellyfish."
- Jellyfish have six body parts, / but / they don't have brains.
- People must protect jellyfish, / for / they are fragile creatures.

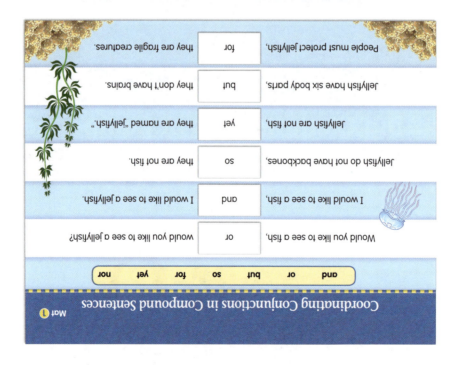

Mat 2 — Coordinating Conjunctions in Compound Sentences

Use a coordinating conjunction to join two simple sentences and make a compound sentence.

- Earth is not like any other planet. Earth has oceans.
  → Earth is not like any other planet, **for** Earth has oceans.
- You can see Earth's oceans by land. You can see them by sea.
  → You can see Earth's oceans by land, **or** you can see them by sea.
- The oceans give us air. They give us food.
  → The oceans give us air, **and** they give us food.
- Salt water fills the oceans. People cannot drink salt water.
  → Salt water fills the oceans, **but** people cannot drink salt water.
- Water covers 70% of Earth's surface. Most people live on land.
  → Water covers 70% of Earth's surface, **yet** most people live on land.

Coordinating Conjunctions in Compound Sentences

Mat 1

| and | or | but | so | for | yet | nor |

- Would you like to see a fish, ___ would you like to see a jellyfish?
- I would like to see a fish, ___ I would like to see a jellyfish.
- Jellyfish do not have backbones, ___ they are not fish.
- Jellyfish are not fish, ___ they are named "jellyfish."
- Jellyfish have six body parts, ___ they don't have brains.
- People must protect jellyfish, ___ they are fragile creatures.

Coordinating Conjunctions in Compound Sentences

Mat 2

Use a coordinating conjunction to join two simple sentences and make a compound sentence.

Earth is not like any other planet. Earth has oceans.

You can see Earth's oceans by land. You can see them by sea.

The oceans give us air. They give us food.

Salt water fills the oceans. People cannot drink salt water.

Water covers 70% of Earth's surface. Most people live on land.

Cards for Mat 1

or	and
so	yet
but	nor
for	but

Cards for Mat 2

Earth is not like any other planet, **for** Earth has oceans.

You can see Earth's oceans by land, **or** you can see them by sea.

The oceans give us air, **and** they give us food.

Salt water fills the oceans, **but** people cannot drink salt water.

Water covers 70% of Earth's surface, **yet** most people live on land.

Coordinating Conjunctions
in Compound Sentences

EMC 2873
© Evan-Moor Corp.

Coordinating Conjunctions
in Compound Sentences

EMC 2873
© Evan-Moor Corp.

Coordinating Conjunctions
in Compound Sentences

EMC 2873
© Evan-Moor Corp.

Coordinating Conjunctions
in Compound Sentences

EMC 2873
© Evan-Moor Corp.

Coordinating Conjunctions
in Compound Sentences

EMC 2873
© Evan-Moor Corp.

Coordinating Conjunctions
in Compound Sentences

EMC 2873
© Evan-Moor Corp.

Coordinating Conjunctions
in Compound Sentences

EMC 2873
© Evan-Moor Corp.

Coordinating Conjunctions
in Compound Sentences

EMC 2873
© Evan-Moor Corp.

Coordinating Conjunctions in Compound Sentences

EMC 2873
© Evan-Moor Corp.

Coordinating Conjunctions in Compound Sentences

EMC 2873
© Evan-Moor Corp.

Coordinating Conjunctions in Compound Sentences

EMC 2873
© Evan-Moor Corp.

Coordinating Conjunctions in Compound Sentences

EMC 2873
© Evan-Moor Corp.

Coordinating Conjunctions in Compound Sentences

EMC 2873
© Evan-Moor Corp.

Take It to Your Seat Centers

Subordinating Conjunctions in Complex Sentences

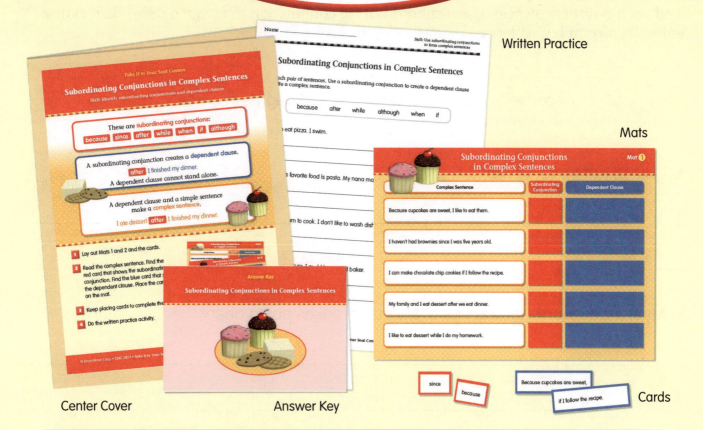

Written Practice

Mats

Center Cover

Answer Key

Cards

CCLS 3.1h, 3.1i Use subordinating conjunctions; produce complex sentences

Skill: Identify subordinating conjunctions and dependent clauses; use subordinating conjunctions to form complex sentences

Steps to Follow

1. **Prepare the center.** (See page 3.)

2. **Introduce the center.** State the goal. Say: *You will identify subordinating conjunctions and dependent clauses and use subordinating conjunctions to form complex sentences.*

3. **Teach the skill.** Demonstrate how to use the center.

4. **Practice the skill.** Have students complete the center tasks independently or with a partner.

Contents

Written Practice..... 98

Center Cover.......... 99

Answer Key............ 101

Center Mats........... 103

Cards..................... 107

Name _____

Skill: Use subordinating conjunctions to form complex sentences

Subordinating Conjunctions in Complex Sentences

Read each pair of sentences. Use a subordinating conjunction to create a dependent clause and write a complex sentence.

> because   after   while   although   when   if

1. I like to eat pizza. I swim.

_____

_____

2. My nana's favorite food is pasta. My nana makes pasta often.

_____

_____

3. I'd like to learn to cook. I don't like to wash dishes.

_____

_____

4. I learn to measure. I could be a good baker.

_____

_____

Take It to Your Seat Centers

Subordinating Conjunctions in Complex Sentences

Skill: Identify subordinating conjunctions and dependent clauses

These are **subordinating conjunctions**:
because **since** **after** **while** **when** **if** **although**

A subordinating conjunction creates a **dependent clause**.

after I finished my dinner.

A dependent clause cannot stand alone.

A dependent clause and a simple sentence make a **complex sentence**.

I ate dessert **after** I finished my dinner.

1 Lay out Mats 1 and 2 and the cards.

2 Read the complex sentence. Find the red card that shows the subordinating conjunction. Find the blue card that shows the dependent clause. Place the cards on the mat.

3 Keep placing cards to complete the mats.

4 Do the written practice activity.

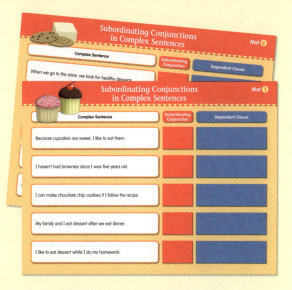

© Evan-Moor Corp. • EMC 2873 • Take It to Your Seat Centers—Language   **Center Cover**

Written Practice

Subordinating Conjunctions in Complex Sentences

Read each pair of sentences. Use a subordinating conjunction to create a dependent clause and write a complex sentence.

because   when   although   while   after   if

Answers will vary—Examples:

1. I like to eat pizza. I swim.
   I like to eat pizza after I swim.

2. My nana's favorite food is pasta. My nana makes pasta often.
   Because my nana's favorite food is pasta, my nana makes pasta often.

3. I'd like to learn to cook. I don't like to wash dishes.
   I'd like to learn to cook although I don't like to wash dishes.

4. I learn to measure. I could be a good baker.
   If I learn to measure, I could be a good baker.

Answer Key

Subordinating Conjunctions in Complex Sentences

Answer Key

Subordinating Conjunctions in Complex Sentences

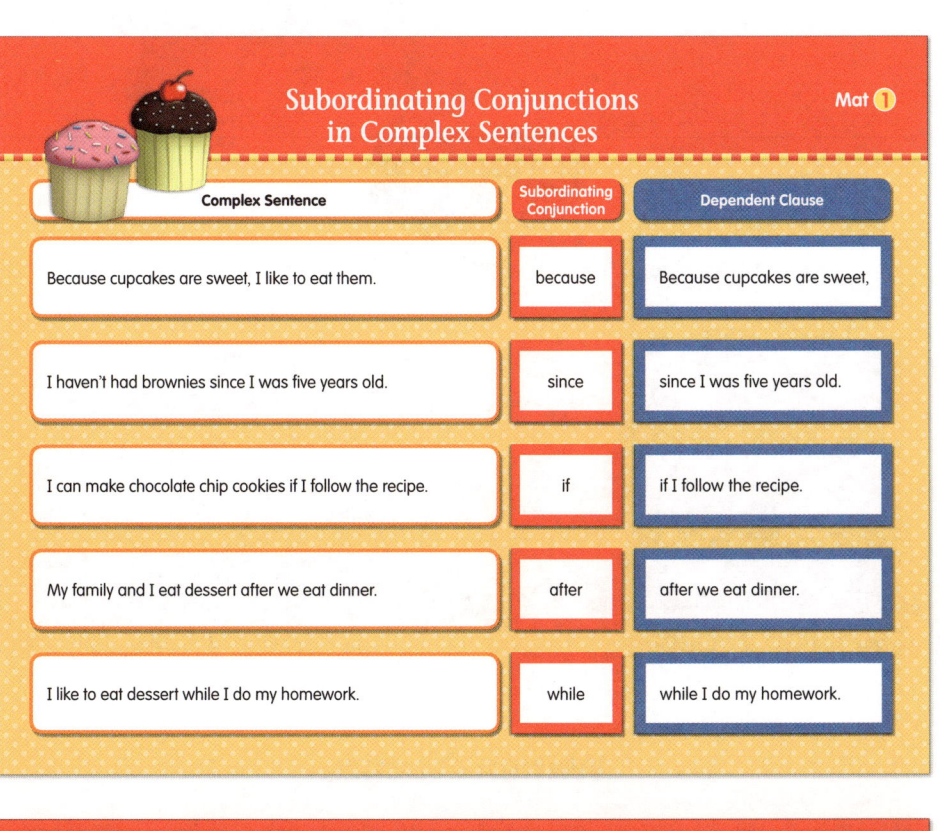

Subordinating Conjunctions in Complex Sentences — Mat 1

Complex Sentence	Subordinating Conjunction	Dependent Clause
Because cupcakes are sweet, I like to eat them.	because	Because cupcakes are sweet,
I haven't had brownies since I was five years old.	since	since I was five years old.
I can make chocolate chip cookies if I follow the recipe.	if	if I follow the recipe.
My family and I eat dessert after we eat dinner.	after	after we eat dinner.
I like to eat dessert while I do my homework.	while	while I do my homework.

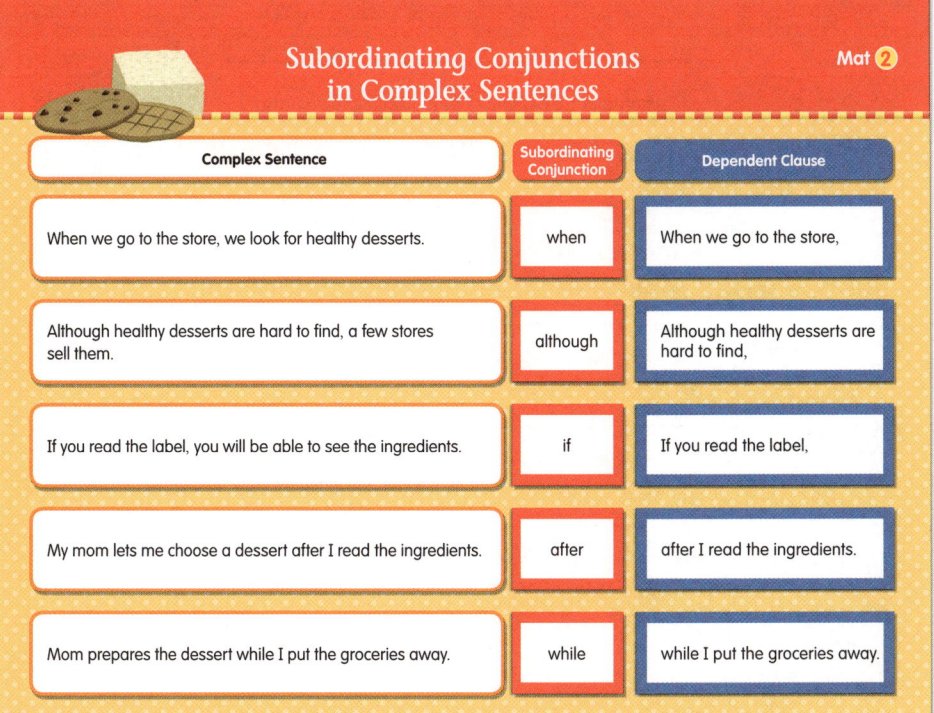

Subordinating Conjunctions in Complex Sentences — Mat 2

Complex Sentence	Subordinating Conjunction	Dependent Clause
When we go to the store, we look for healthy desserts.	when	When we go to the store,
Although healthy desserts are hard to find, a few stores sell them.	although	Although healthy desserts are hard to find,
If you read the label, you will be able to see the ingredients.	if	If you read the label,
My mom lets me choose a dessert after I read the ingredients.	after	after I read the ingredients.
Mom prepares the dessert while I put the groceries away.	while	while I put the groceries away.

Subordinating Conjunctions in Complex Sentences

Mat 1

Dependent Clause	Subordinating Conjunction	Complex Sentence
		Because cupcakes are sweet, I like to eat them.
		I haven't had brownies since I was five years old.
		I can make chocolate chip cookies if I follow the recipe.
		My family and I eat dessert after we eat dinner.
		I like to eat dessert while I do my homework.

Subordinating Conjunctions in Complex Sentences

Mat 2

Dependent Clause	Subordinating Conjunction	Complex Sentence
		When we go to the store, we look for healthy desserts.
		Although healthy desserts are hard to find, a few stores sell them.
		If you read the label, you will be able to see the ingredients.
		My mom lets me choose a dessert after I read the ingredients.
		Mom prepares the dessert while I put the groceries away.

Cards for Mats 1 and 2

because	since	if	after	while
when	although	if	after	while

Because cupcakes are sweet,	since I was five years old.
if I follow the recipe.	after we eat dinner.
while I do my homework.	When we go to the store,
Although healthy desserts are hard to find,	If you read the label,
after I read the ingredients.	while I put the groceries away.

Subordinating Conjunctions in Complex Sentences

EMC 2873
© Evan-Moor Corp.

Subordinating Conjunctions in Complex Sentences

EMC 2873
© Evan-Moor Corp.

Subordinating Conjunctions in Complex Sentences

EMC 2873
© Evan-Moor Corp.

Subordinating Conjunctions in Complex Sentences

EMC 2873
© Evan-Moor Corp.

Subordinating Conjunctions in Complex Sentences

EMC 2873
© Evan-Moor Corp.

Subordinating Conjunctions in Complex Sentences

EMC 2873
© Evan-Moor Corp.

Subordinating Conjunctions in Complex Sentences

EMC 2873
© Evan-Moor Corp.

Subordinating Conjunctions in Complex Sentences

EMC 2873
© Evan-Moor Corp.

Subordinating Conjunctions in Complex Sentences

EMC 2873
© Evan-Moor Corp.

Subordinating Conjunctions in Complex Sentences

EMC 2873
© Evan-Moor Corp.

Subordinating Conjunctions in Complex Sentences

EMC 2873 • © Evan-Moor Corp.

Subordinating Conjunctions in Complex Sentences

EMC 2873 • © Evan-Moor Corp.

Subordinating Conjunctions in Complex Sentences

EMC 2873 • © Evan-Moor Corp.

Subordinating Conjunctions in Complex Sentences

EMC 2873 • © Evan-Moor Corp.

Subordinating Conjunctions in Complex Sentences

EMC 2873 • © Evan-Moor Corp.

Subordinating Conjunctions in Complex Sentences

EMC 2873 • © Evan-Moor Corp.

Subordinating Conjunctions in Complex Sentences

EMC 2873 • © Evan-Moor Corp.

Subordinating Conjunctions in Complex Sentences

EMC 2873 • © Evan-Moor Corp.

Subordinating Conjunctions in Complex Sentences

EMC 2873 • © Evan-Moor Corp.

Subordinating Conjunctions in Complex Sentences

EMC 2873 • © Evan-Moor Corp.

Take It to Your Seat Centers

Affixes

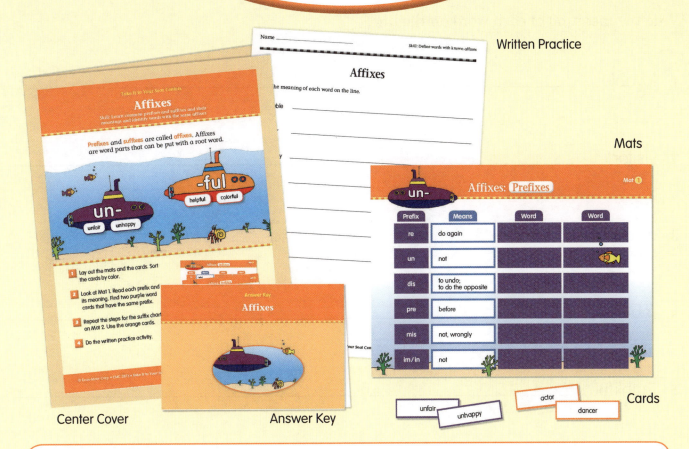

CCLS 3.4b Determine the meaning of the new word formed when a known affix is added to a known word

Skill: Learn common prefixes and suffixes and their meanings and identify words with the same affixes; define words with known affixes

Steps to Follow

1. **Prepare the center.** (See page 3.)
2. **Introduce the center.** State the goal. Say: *You will make new words by matching prefix and suffix cards with root words.*
3. **Teach the skill.** Demonstrate how to use the center.
4. **Practice the skill.** Have students complete the center tasks independently or with a partner.

Contents

Written Practice..... 110
Center Cover.......... 111
Answer Key............ 113
Center Mats........... 115
Cards..................... 119

Name _____

Skill: Define words with known affixes

Affixes

Write the meaning of each word on the line.

1. lovable _____

2. visitor _____

3. disobey _____

4. rebuild _____

5. thankful _____

6. preplan _____

7. tasteless _____

Take It to Your Seat Centers

Affixes

Skill: Learn common prefixes and suffixes and their meanings and identify words with the same affixes

Prefixes and **suffixes** are called **affixes**. Affixes are word parts that can be put with a root word.

1. Lay out the mats and the cards. Sort the cards by color.

2. Look at Mat 1. Read each prefix and its meaning. Find two purple word cards that have the same prefix.

3. Repeat the steps for the suffix chart on Mat 2. Use the orange cards.

4. Do the written practice activity.

Written Practice

Affixes

Name _____

Write the meaning of each word on the line.

1. lovable — can be loved
2. visitor — a person who visits
3. disobey — to do the opposite of obeying
4. rebuild — to build again
5. thankful — full of thanks
6. preplan — to plan before
7. tasteless — without taste

Answer Key

Affixes

Answer Key
Affixes

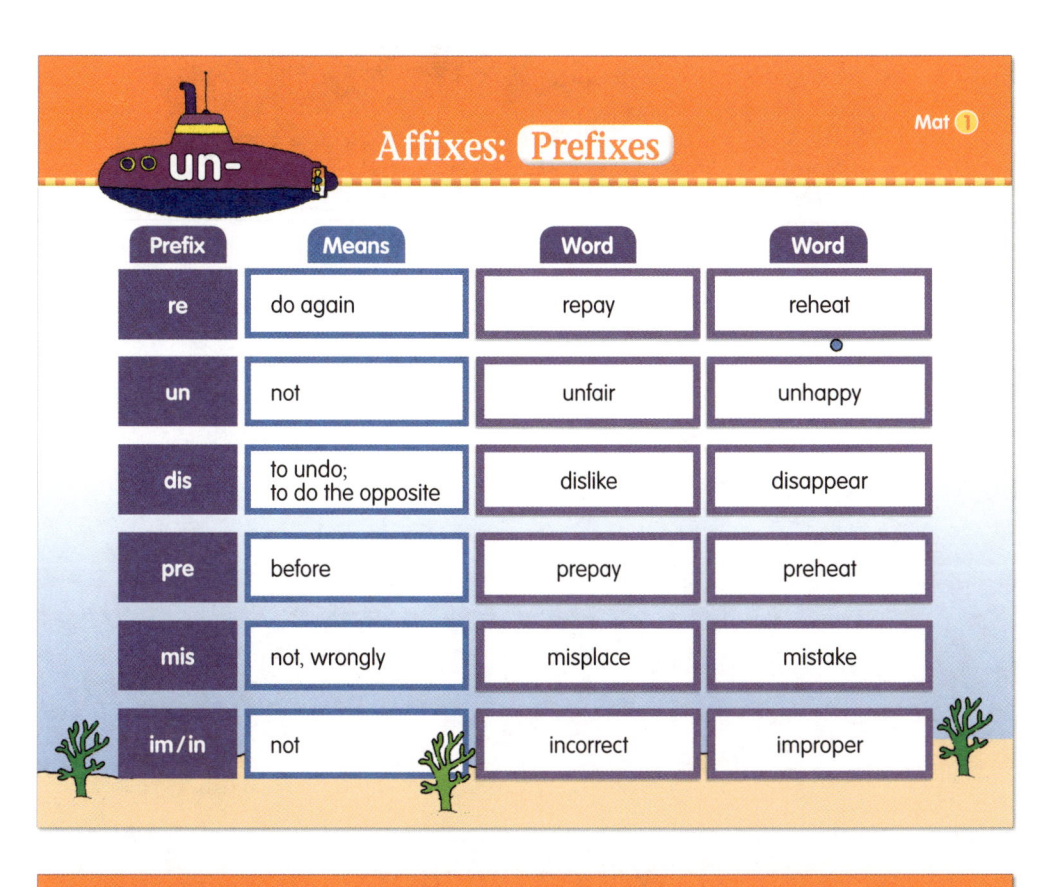

Affixes: Prefixes   Mat 1

Prefix	Means	Word	Word
re	do again	repay	reheat
un	not	unfair	unhappy
dis	to undo; to do the opposite	dislike	disappear
pre	before	prepay	preheat
mis	not, wrongly	misplace	mistake
im/in	not	incorrect	improper

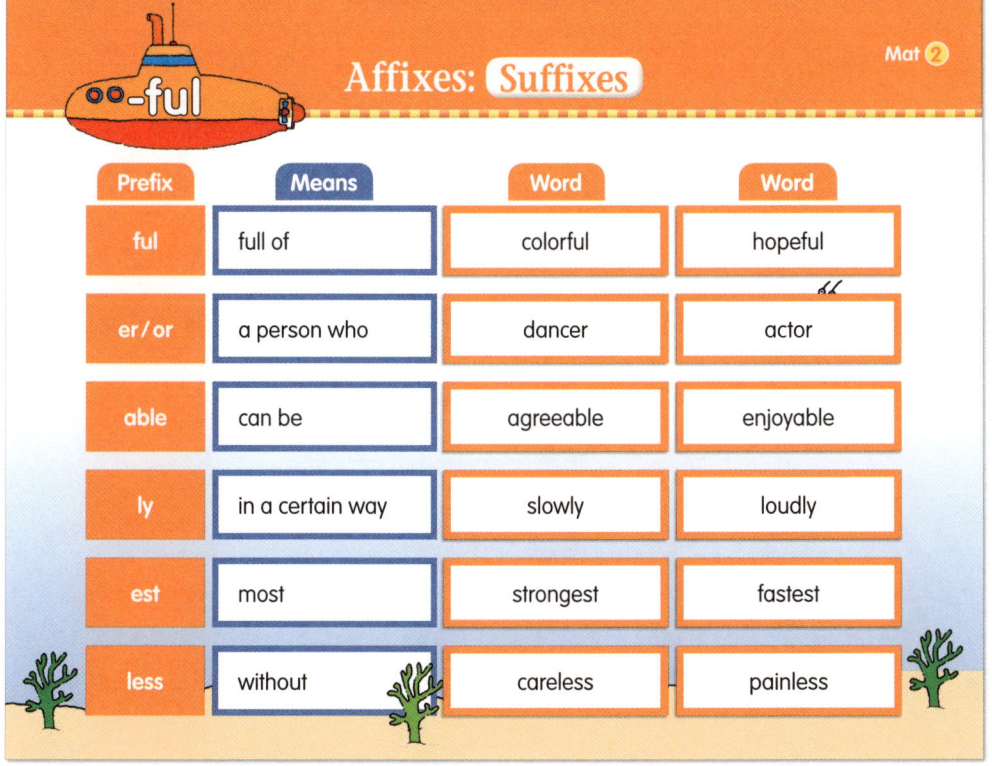

Affixes: Suffixes   Mat 2

Prefix	Means	Word	Word
ful	full of	colorful	hopeful
er/or	a person who	dancer	actor
able	can be	agreeable	enjoyable
ly	in a certain way	slowly	loudly
est	most	strongest	fastest
less	without	careless	painless

Affixes: Prefixes

Prefix	Means	Word	Word
re	do again		
un	not		
dis	to undo; to do the opposite		
pre	before		
mis	not, wrongly		
im/in	not		

Mat 1

un-

Mat 2

Affixes: Suffixes

Prefix	Means	Word	Word
ful	full of		
er/or	a person who		
able	can be		
ly	in a certain way		
est	most		
less	without		

Cards for Mat 1

repay	reheat	unfair
unhappy	dislike	disappear
prepay	preheat	misplace
mistake	incorrect	improper

Cards for Mat 2

colorful	hopeful	dancer
actor	agreeable	enjoyable
slowly	loudly	strongest
fastest	careless	painless

Affixes	**Affixes**	**Affixes**
EMC 2873	EMC 2873	EMC 2873
© Evan-Moor Corp.	© Evan-Moor Corp.	© Evan-Moor Corp.

Affixes	**Affixes**	**Affixes**
EMC 2873	EMC 2873	EMC 2873
© Evan-Moor Corp.	© Evan-Moor Corp.	© Evan-Moor Corp.

Affixes	**Affixes**	**Affixes**
EMC 2873	EMC 2873	EMC 2873
© Evan-Moor Corp.	© Evan-Moor Corp.	© Evan-Moor Corp.

Affixes	**Affixes**	**Affixes**
EMC 2873	EMC 2873	EMC 2873
© Evan-Moor Corp.	© Evan-Moor Corp.	© Evan-Moor Corp.

Affixes	**Affixes**	**Affixes**
EMC 2873	EMC 2873	EMC 2873
© Evan-Moor Corp.	© Evan-Moor Corp.	© Evan-Moor Corp.

Affixes	**Affixes**	**Affixes**
EMC 2873	EMC 2873	EMC 2873
© Evan-Moor Corp.	© Evan-Moor Corp.	© Evan-Moor Corp.

Affixes	**Affixes**	**Affixes**
EMC 2873	EMC 2873	EMC 2873
© Evan-Moor Corp.	© Evan-Moor Corp.	© Evan-Moor Corp.

Affixes	**Affixes**	**Affixes**
EMC 2873	EMC 2873	EMC 2873
© Evan-Moor Corp.	© Evan-Moor Corp.	© Evan-Moor Corp.

Take It to Your Seat Centers

Root Words

Center Cover Answer Key Cards

CCLS 3.4c Use a known root word as a clue to the meaning of an unknown word with the same root

Skill: Match definitions to root words; identify word roots in words and use the words in context sentences

Steps to Follow

1. **Prepare the center.** (See page 3.)
2. **Introduce the center.** State the goal. Say: *You will read root words with and without definitions. You will match definition cards to the root words that do not have definitions.*
3. **Teach the skill.** Demonstrate how to use the center.
4. **Practice the skill.** Have students complete the center tasks independently or with a partner.

Contents

Written Practice..... 122

Center Cover.......... 123

Answer Key............ 125

Center Mats 127

Cards 131

Name _____

Skill: Identify word roots in words and use the words in context sentences

Root Words

Read each word. Look for the root. Write the word root on the line.

1. transportation _____
2. pedestrian _____
3. remote _____
4. community _____

5. biology _____
6. active _____
7. stethoscope _____
8. homograph _____

Complete each sentence using a word from above. Write the word on the line.

9. A bike that moves fast is my favorite kind of _____.

10. My doctor used a _____ to listen to my heart beat.

11. My dog can do a lot of tricks and is always _____.

12. On my street, we all get together and have a _____ party.

13. The word **bat** is a _____ because it has different meanings but is spelled the same.

14. A person crossing the street is called a _____.

Take It to Your Seat Centers

Root Words

Skill: Match definitions to root words

A **word root** is a word part that has a meaning of its own.

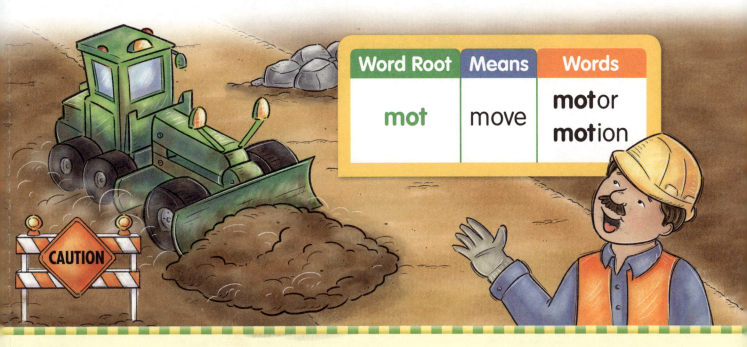

1. Lay out the mats and the cards.

2. Look at row 1. Read the root and its meaning in the first box.

3. In the second box, read the root word and its definition.

4. In the third box, read the green word. Find its definition card and place it on the mat.

5. Keep placing cards until the mats are complete.

6. Do the written practice activity.

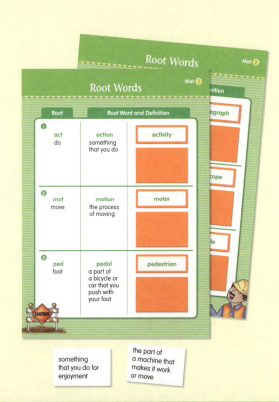

© Evan-Moor Corp. • EMC 2873 • Take It to Your Seat Centers—Language

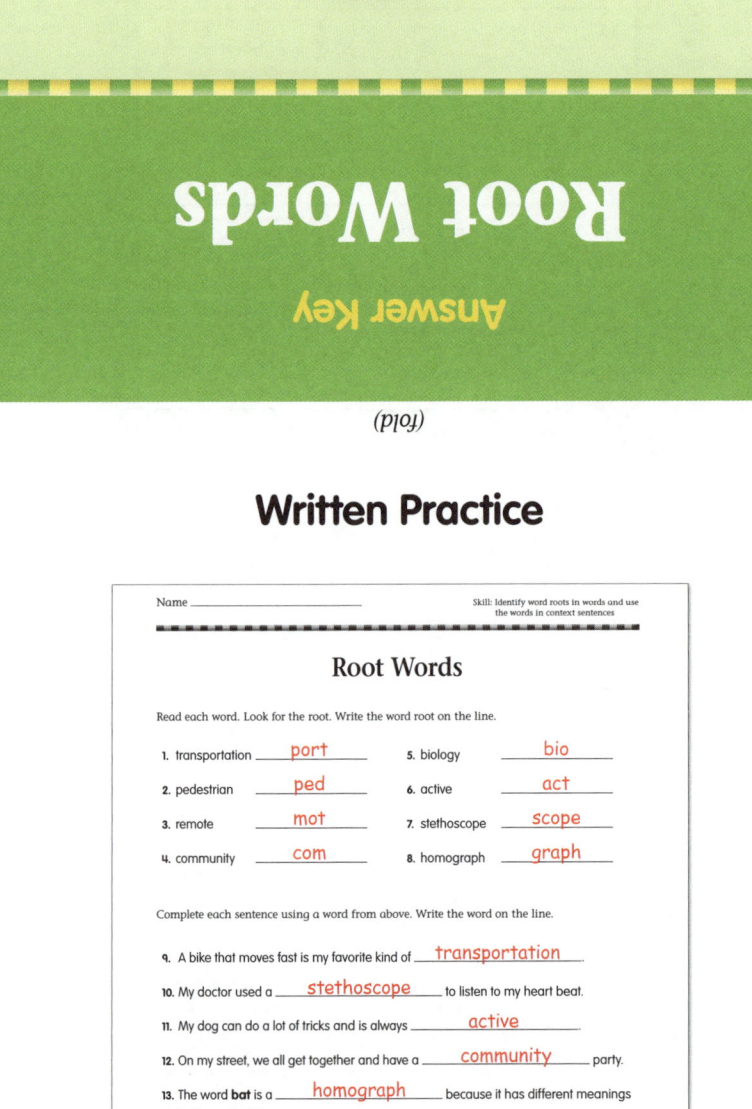

Root Words

Answer Key

(fold)

Written Practice

Name _____

Skill: Identify word roots in words and use the words in context sentences

Root Words

Read each word. Look for the root. Write the word root on the line.

1. transportation ___port___
2. pedestrian ___ped___
3. remote ___mot___
4. community ___com___
5. biology ___bio___
6. active ___act___
7. stethoscope ___scope___
8. homograph ___graph___

Complete each sentence using a word from above. Write the word on the line.

9. A bike that moves fast is my favorite kind of ___transportation___
10. My doctor used a ___stethoscope___ to listen to my heart beat.
11. My dog can do a lot of tricks and is always ___active___
12. On my street, we all get together and have a ___community___ party.
13. The word **bat** is a ___homograph___ because it has different meanings but is spelled the same.
14. A person crossing the street is called a ___pedestrian___

122 Written Practice   Take It to Your Seat Centers—Language • EMC 2873 • © Evan-Moor Corp.

Take It to Your Seat Centers—Language • EMC 2873 • © Evan-Moor Corp.

Answer Key
Root Words

Mat 1

Root	Root Word and Definition	
1	act — do	action — something that you do	**activity** — something that you do for enjoyment
2	mot — move	motion — the process of moving	**motor** — the part of a machine that makes it work or move
3	ped — foot	pedal — a part of a bicycle or car that you push with your foot	**pedestrian** — someone who is walking in a town

Mat 2

Root	Root Word and Definition	
4	graph — write or draw	autograph — a famous person's name, written by him or her	**paragraph** — a group of sentences in a piece of writing
5	scope — watch or see	microscope — an instrument that helps you see small things by making them look bigger	**telescope** — an instrument that makes things that are far away look closer
6	port — carry	import — to bring things into a country to sell or use	**portable** — light and easy to move or carry

Root Words

Mat 1

Root	Root Word and Definition	
1 **act** do	**action** something that you do	**activity**
2 **mot** move	**motion** the process of moving	**motor**
3 **ped** foot	**pedal** a part of a bicycle or car that you push with your foot	**pedestrian**

Root Words

Mat 2

Root	Root Word and Definition	
4 **graph** write or draw	**autograph** a famous person's name, written by him or her	**paragraph**
5 **scope** watch or see	**microscope** an instrument that helps you see small things by making them look bigger	**telescope**
6 **port** carry	**import** to bring things into a country to sell or use	**portable**

Cards for Mats 1 and 2

something that you do for enjoyment	a group of sentences in a piece of writing
the part of a machine that makes it work or move	an instrument that makes things that are far away look closer
someone who is walking in a town	light and easy to move or carry

Root Words	Root Words
EMC 2873	EMC 2873
© Evan-Moor Corp.	© Evan-Moor Corp.

Root Words	Root Words
EMC 2873	EMC 2873
© Evan-Moor Corp.	© Evan-Moor Corp.

Root Words	Root Words
EMC 2873	EMC 2873
© Evan-Moor Corp.	© Evan-Moor Corp.

Take It to Your Seat Centers

Words in Real Life

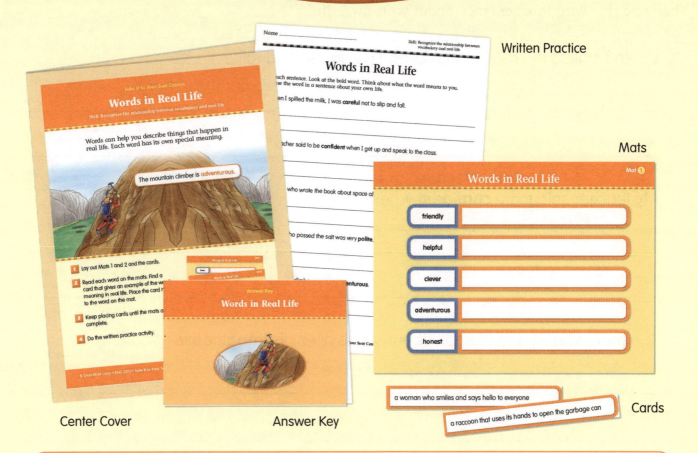

Center Cover Answer Key Cards

CCLS **3.5b** Identify real-life connections between words and their use

Skill: Recognize the relationship between vocabulary and real life

Steps to Follow

1. **Prepare the center.** (See page 3.)

2. **Introduce the center.** State the goal. Say: *You will read a word and find a card that gives an example of the word's meaning.*

3. **Teach the skill.** Demonstrate how to use the center.

4. **Practice the skill.** Have students complete the center tasks independently or with a partner.

Contents

Written Practice..... 134

Center Cover.......... 135

Answer Key............ 137

Center Mats........... 139

Cards..................... 143

Name _____

Skill: Recognize the relationship between vocabulary and real life

Words in Real Life

Read each sentence. Look at the bold word. Think about what the word means to you. Then use the word in a sentence about your own life.

1. When I spilled the milk, I was **careful** not to slip and fall.

   _____
   _____

2. My teacher said to be **confident** when I get up and speak to the class.

   _____
   _____

3. The man who wrote the book about space aliens is **imaginative**.

   _____
   _____

4. The child who passed the salt was very **polite**.

   _____
   _____

5. The mountain climber was very **adventurous**.

   _____
   _____

Take It to Your Seat Centers

Words in Real Life

Skill: Recognize the relationship between vocabulary and real life

Words can help you describe things that happen in real life. Each word has its own special meaning.

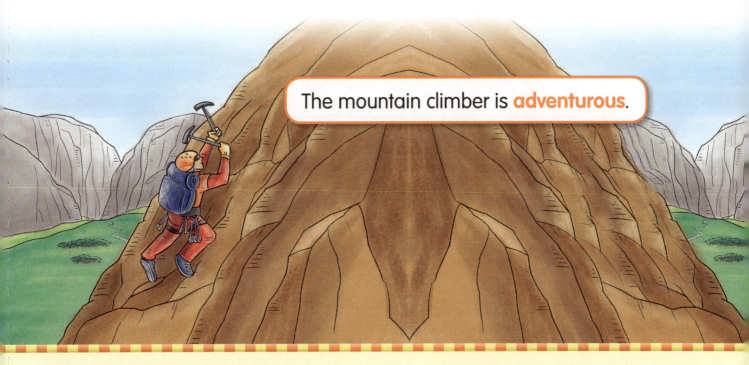

The mountain climber is **adventurous**.

1. Lay out Mats 1 and 2 and the cards.

2. Read each word on the mats. Find a card that gives an example of the word's meaning in real life. Place the card next to the word on the mat.

3. Keep placing cards until the mats are complete.

4. Do the written practice activity.

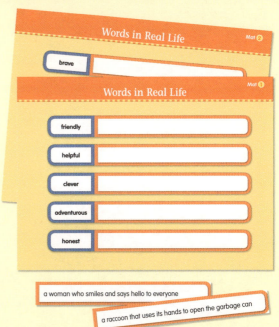

Written Practice

Words in Real Life

Name _____

Skill: Recognize the relationship between vocabulary and real life

Read each sentence. Look at the bold word. Think about what the word means to you. Then use the word in a sentence about your own life.

Answers will vary.

1. When I spilled the milk, I was **careful** not to slip and fall.

2. My teacher said to be **confident** when I get up and speak to the class.

3. The man who wrote the book about space aliens is **imaginative**.

4. The child who passed the salt was very **polite**.

5. The mountain climber was very **adventurous**.

(fold)

Answer Key

Words in Real Life

Answer Key

Words in Real Life

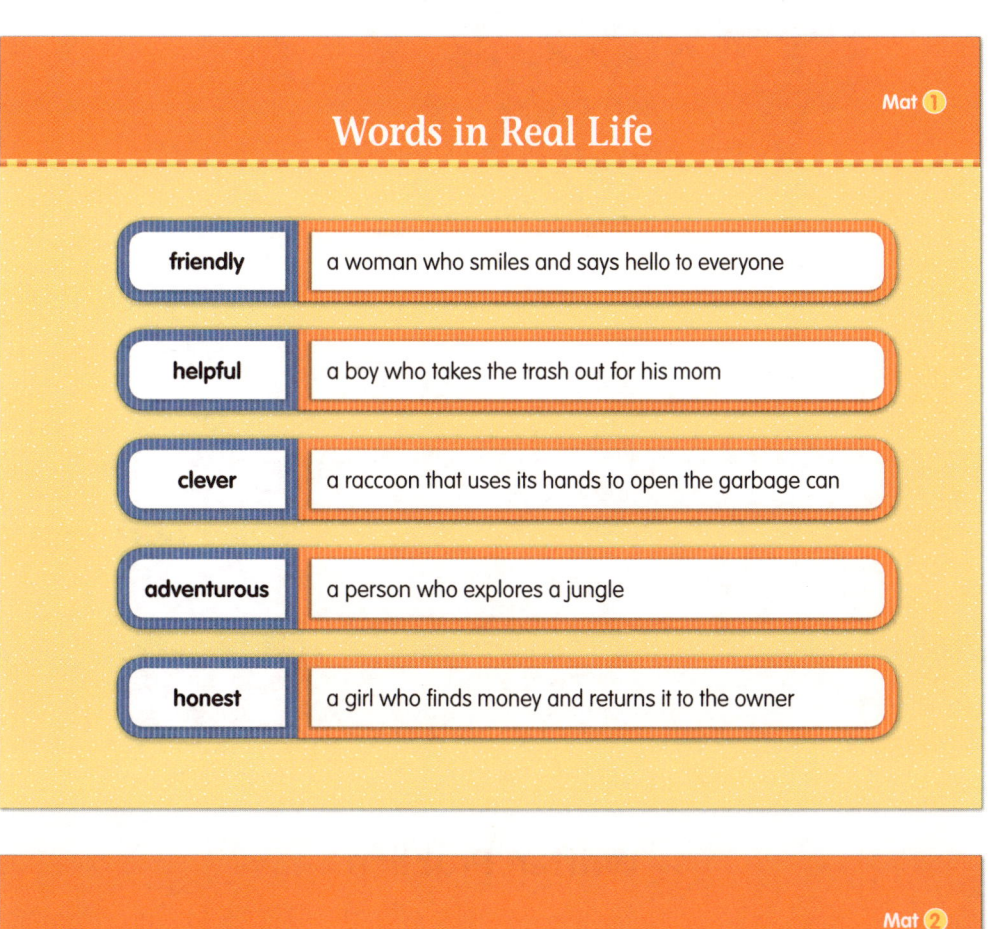

Words in Real Life
Mat 1

friendly	a woman who smiles and says hello to everyone
helpful	a boy who takes the trash out for his mom
clever	a raccoon that uses its hands to open the garbage can
adventurous	a person who explores a jungle
honest	a girl who finds money and returns it to the owner

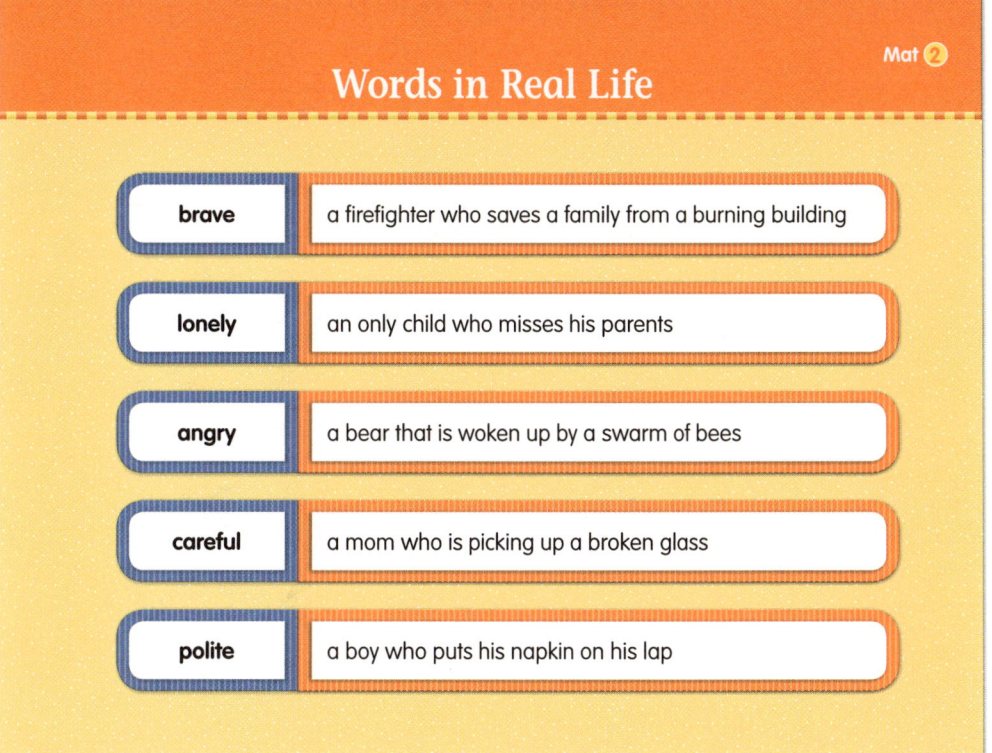

Words in Real Life
Mat 2

brave	a firefighter who saves a family from a burning building
lonely	an only child who misses his parents
angry	a bear that is woken up by a swarm of bees
careful	a mom who is picking up a broken glass
polite	a boy who puts his napkin on his lap

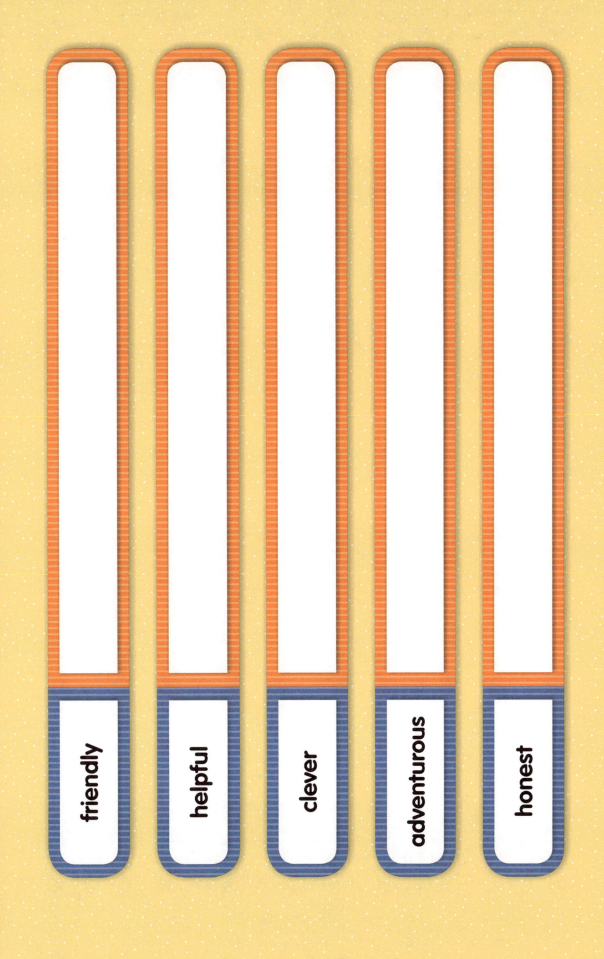

Words in Real Life

Mat 2

- brave
- lonely
- angry
- careful
- polite

Cards for Mats 1 and 2

- a woman who smiles and says hello to everyone
- a boy who takes the trash out for his mom
- a raccoon that uses its hands to open the garbage can
- a person who explores a jungle
- a girl who finds money and returns it to the owner
- a firefighter who saves a family from a burning building
- an only child who misses his parents
- a bear that is woken up by a swarm of bees
- a mom who is picking up a broken glass
- a boy who puts his napkin on his lap

Words in Real Life
EMC 2873
© Evan-Moor Corp.

Words in Real Life
EMC 2873
© Evan-Moor Corp.

Words in Real Life
EMC 2873
© Evan-Moor Corp.

Words in Real Life
EMC 2873
© Evan-Moor Corp.

Words in Real Life
EMC 2873
© Evan-Moor Corp.

Words in Real Life
EMC 2873
© Evan-Moor Corp.

Words in Real Life
EMC 2873
© Evan-Moor Corp.

Words in Real Life
EMC 2873
© Evan-Moor Corp.

Words in Real Life
EMC 2873
© Evan-Moor Corp.

Words in Real Life
EMC 2873
© Evan-Moor Corp.

Take It to Your Seat Centers

Shades of Meaning

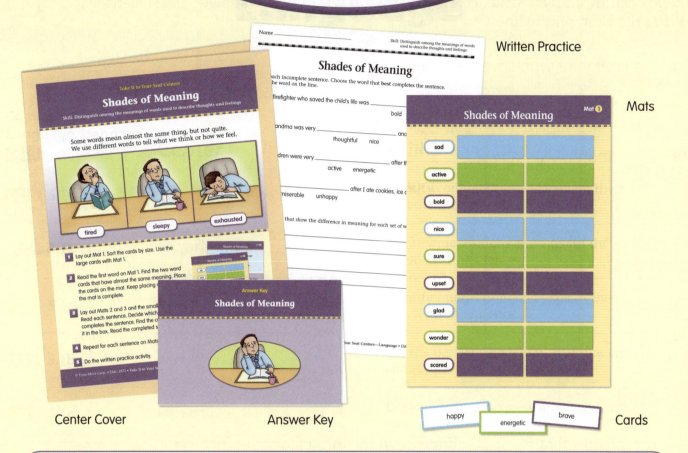

Written Practice

Mats

Center Cover

Answer Key

Cards

CCLS 3.5c Distinguish shades of meaning among related words that describe states of mind or degrees of certainty

Skill: Distinguish among the meanings of words used to describe thoughts and feelings

Steps to Follow

1. **Prepare the center.** (See page 3.)

2. **Introduce the center.** State the goal. Say: *You will identify words that have similar meanings and choose words with the most precise meanings.*

3. **Teach the skill.** Demonstrate how to use the center.

4. **Practice the skill.** Have students complete the center tasks independently or with a partner.

Contents

Written Practice..... 146

Center Cover.......... 147

Answer Key............ 149

Center Mats........... 151

Cards 157

Teacher Instructions

Name _____

Skill: Distinguish among the meanings of words used to describe thoughts and feelings

Shades of Meaning

Read each incomplete sentence. Choose the word that **best** completes the sentence. Write the word on the line.

1. The firefighter who saved the child's life was _____.

   bold   heroic

2. My grandma was very _____ and sent me a get-well card.

   thoughtful   nice

3. The children were very _____ after they ate a sugary snack.

   active   energetic

4. I felt _____ after I ate cookies, ice cream, *and* cake.

   miserable   unhappy

Write sentences that show the difference in meaning for each set of words.

5. upset _____

   angry _____

6. surprised _____

   amazed _____

Take It to Your Seat Centers

Shades of Meaning

Skill: Distinguish among the meanings of words used to describe thoughts and feelings

Some words mean almost the same thing, but not quite. We use different words to tell what we think or how we feel.

tired   sleepy   exhausted

1. Lay out Mat 1. Sort the cards by size. Use the large cards with Mat 1.

2. Read the first word on Mat 1. Find the two word cards that have almost the same meaning. Place the cards on the mat. Keep placing cards until the mat is complete.

3. Lay out Mats 2 and 3 and the small cards. Read each sentence. Decide which word best completes the sentence. Find the card and place it in the box. Read the completed sentence.

4. Repeat for each sentence on Mats 2 and 3.

5. Do the written practice activity.

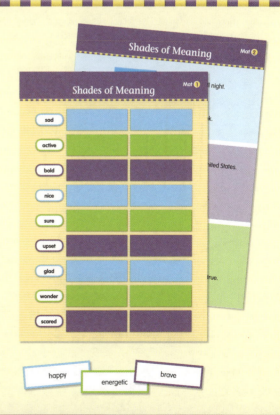

Name _____

Shades of Meaning

Read each incomplete sentence. Choose the word that best completes the sentence. Write the word on the line.

1. The firefighter who saved the child's life was ___**heroic**___.
   bold heroic

2. My grandma was very ___**thoughtful**___ and sent me a get-well card.
   nice thoughtful

3. The children were very ___**energetic**___ after they ate a sugary snack.
   active energetic

4. I felt ___**miserable**___ after I ate cookies, ice cream, and cake.
   unhappy miserable

Write sentences that show the difference in meaning for each set of words. **Answers will vary.**

5. upset _____
   angry _____

6. surprised _____
   amazed _____

Written Practice

(fold)

Answer Key

Shades of Meaning

Answer Key
Shades of Meaning

Shades of Meaning — Mat 1

scared	frightened	terrified
wonder	think about	curious
glad	happy	thrilled
upset	angry	furious
sure	confident	positive
nice	thoughtful	kind
bold	brave	heroic
active	energetic	lively
sad	unhappy	miserable

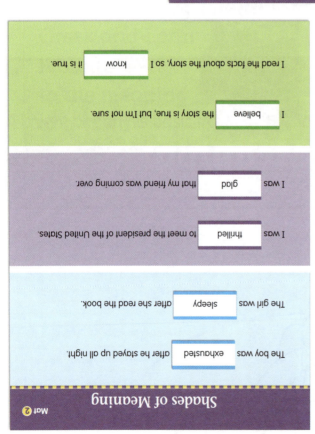

Shades of Meaning — Mat 2

The boy was **exhausted** after he stayed up all night.

The girl was **sleepy** after she read the book.

I was **thrilled** to meet the president of the United States.

I was **glad** that my friend was coming over.

I **believe** the story is true, but I'm not sure.

I **know** the facts about the story, so it is true.

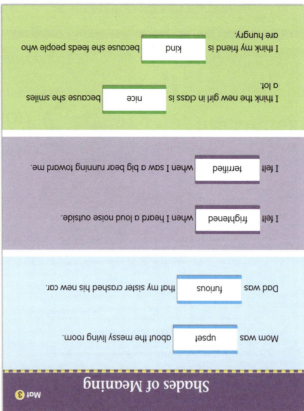

Shades of Meaning — Mat 3

Mom was **upset** about the messy living room.

Dad was **furious** that my sister crashed his new car.

I felt **frightened** when I heard a loud noise outside.

I felt **terrified** when I saw a big bear running toward me.

I think the new girl in class is **nice** because she smiles a lot.

I think my friend is **kind** because she feeds people who are hungry.

Shades of Meaning

Mat 1

- sad
- active
- bold
- nice
- sure
- upset
- glad
- wonder
- scared

Shades of Meaning

Mat 2

The boy was [exhausted / sleepy] after he stayed up all night.

The girl was [exhausted / sleepy] after she read the book.

I was [glad / thrilled] to meet the president of the United States.

I was [glad / thrilled] that my friend was coming over.

I [know / believe] the story is true, but I'm not sure.

I read the facts about the story, so I [know / believe] it is true.

Shades of Meaning

Mat 3

Mom was [upset / furious] about the messy living room.

Dad was [upset / furious] that my sister crashed his new car.

I felt [frightened / terrified] when I heard a loud noise outside.

I felt [frightened / terrified] when I saw a big bear running toward me.

I think the new girl in class is [nice / kind] because she smiles a lot.

I think my friend is [nice / kind] because she feeds people who are hungry.

Cards for Mat 1

unhappy	miserable
thoughtful	kind
happy	thrilled
energetic	lively
confident	positive
think about	curious
brave	heroic
angry	furious
frightened	terrified

Shades of Meaning	Shades of Meaning
EMC 2873	EMC 2873
© Evan-Moor Corp.	© Evan-Moor Corp.

Shades of Meaning	Shades of Meaning
EMC 2873	EMC 2873
© Evan-Moor Corp.	© Evan-Moor Corp.

Shades of Meaning	Shades of Meaning
EMC 2873	EMC 2873
© Evan-Moor Corp.	© Evan-Moor Corp.

Shades of Meaning	Shades of Meaning
EMC 2873	EMC 2873
© Evan-Moor Corp.	© Evan-Moor Corp.

Shades of Meaning	Shades of Meaning
EMC 2873	EMC 2873
© Evan-Moor Corp.	© Evan-Moor Corp.

Shades of Meaning	Shades of Meaning
EMC 2873	EMC 2873
© Evan-Moor Corp.	© Evan-Moor Corp.

Shades of Meaning	Shades of Meaning
EMC 2873	EMC 2873
© Evan-Moor Corp.	© Evan-Moor Corp.

Shades of Meaning	Shades of Meaning
EMC 2873	EMC 2873
© Evan-Moor Corp.	© Evan-Moor Corp.

Shades of Meaning	Shades of Meaning
EMC 2873	EMC 2873
© Evan-Moor Corp.	© Evan-Moor Corp.

Cards for Mats 2 and 3

exhausted	sleepy
upset	furious
thrilled	glad
frightened	terrified
believe	know
nice	kind

Shades of Meaning	Shades of Meaning
EMC 2873	EMC 2873
© Evan-Moor Corp.	© Evan-Moor Corp.
Shades of Meaning	Shades of Meaning
EMC 2873	EMC 2873
© Evan-Moor Corp.	© Evan-Moor Corp.
Shades of Meaning	Shades of Meaning
EMC 2873	EMC 2873
© Evan-Moor Corp.	© Evan-Moor Corp.
Shades of Meaning	Shades of Meaning
EMC 2873	EMC 2873
© Evan-Moor Corp.	© Evan-Moor Corp.
Shades of Meaning	Shades of Meaning
EMC 2873	EMC 2873
© Evan-Moor Corp.	© Evan-Moor Corp.
Shades of Meaning	Shades of Meaning
EMC 2873	EMC 2873
© Evan-Moor Corp.	© Evan-Moor Corp.